THE FLAVOR OF Upstate New York

THE FLAVOR OF Upstate New York

Iconic Dishes,
Delicious History
& Reinvented
Recipes

JUNE HERSH

Published by American Palate
A division of The History Press
An imprint of Arcadia Publishing
Charleston, SC
www.historypress.com

First published 2025

Manufactured in the United States

ISBN 9781467170062

Library of Congress Control Number: 2025933742

Notice: The information in this book is true and complete to the best of our knowledge. It is offered without guarantee on the part of the author or The History Press. The author and The History Press disclaim all liability in connection with the use of this book.

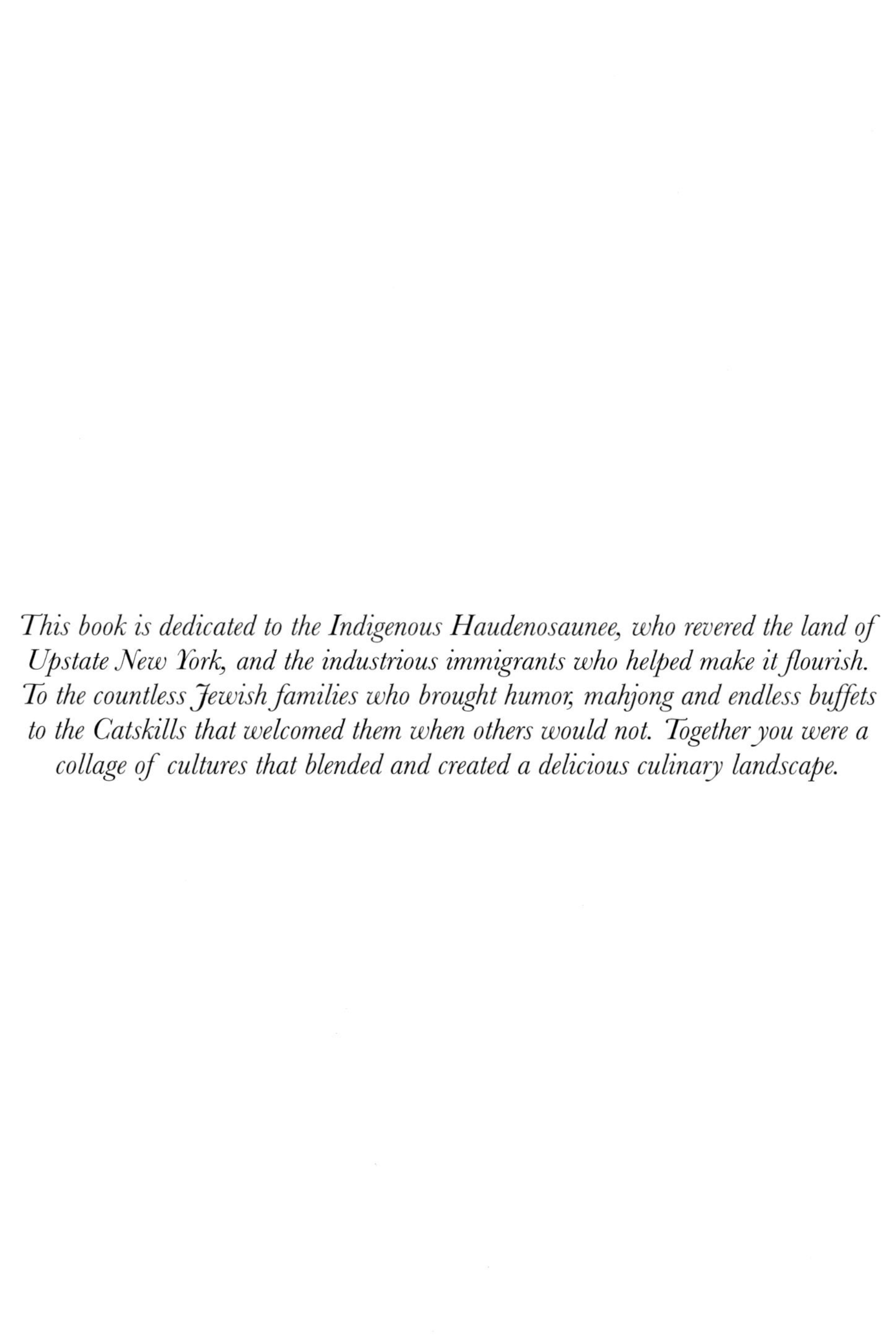

This book is dedicated to the Indigenous Haudenosaunee, who revered the land of Upstate New York, and the industrious immigrants who helped make it flourish. To the countless Jewish families who brought humor, mahjong and endless buffets to the Catskills that welcomed them when others would not. Together you were a collage of cultures that blended and created a delicious culinary landscape.

CONTENTS

ACKNOWLEDGEMENTS

Writing a book about Upstate New York was a trip, and I mean that literally, because you cannot appreciate all the region has to offer without going there and experiencing it for yourself. So, thank you to the shopkeepers, bartenders, pizza makers, sauce gurus, bakers, purveyors and all the dedicated foodies whose restaurants and establishments welcomed me to sample the diverse offerings that represent Upstate New York.

I have not written a book since my first in 2011 in which I do not thank Andrew F. Smith, my literary guardian. Without you I would not know the great satisfaction in discovering food history. Thank you to Derrick Pratt for your time, materials and video tutorials related to the Erie Canal; you are a font of information and were so helpful with that chapter. Derrick is to the Erie Canal what Susan Eck is to the Pan-American Exposition; her resources and information were invaluable. Thera Clarke, a toast to you and all you shared about the Finger Lakes wine industry. It was intoxicating to hear all the developments in this beautiful part of the state. The team at The History Press continues to impress. Banks Smither, you have been a fierce advocate and a pleasure to work with on this, our third project together. Thank you for assembling a great group who did the heavy lifting, including editor Abigail Fleming.

No book I work on can be completed without the support of my family and friends. You listened to my travelogue and deep dive into the culinary curiosities I encountered and showed interest and excitement (even when

I might have droned on about the origin of granola). My final thank-you, which is greater than the ingredients in a garbage plate, is to my husband, Ron, who fearlessly accompanied me on every journey, sampled every dish and read every sentence I wrote. Your love, support and pride in what I do means as much to me as beef on weck means to Buffalo (and that is saying a lot).

As always, I invite you, the reader, to reach out and let me know your thoughts. Without the story, a dish is just ingredients, so please share your stories with me on Instagram @junehersh or via email: junehersh@gmail.com. Hope to pay a visit to your neck of the woods and share a big slice of upside down pizza together.

INTRODUCTION

Food is a preeminent storyteller with a narrative that is more than the sum of its parts. That is especially the case for the diverse foods that have Upstate origins, as they provide insights into the culinary habits of a region that is far more complex than the dishes present. On the surface, Upstate New York food is fun and creative; it's unique and approachable. It is best washed down with a cold beer and friendly conversation. But when you investigate the why behind the what, you find so many layers that tell the full story. Chicken riggies, salt potatoes and beef on weck aren't just local foods; they reflect the resourcefulness of Italian, Irish and German immigrants. When white corn is harvested, it isn't about the kernels but the influence and importance of the Indigenous Haudenosaunee people who first inhabited the region. And when we sprinkle granola on our morning yogurt, we're not just eating healthy, we're eating Upstate history.

Geography is important. It determines your climate, your topography and your agricultural possibilities. Geography is generally precise. The equator is 24,901 miles in circumference and divides the earth into north and south. The Greenwich Meridian lies at 0 degrees longitude and separates the Eastern and Western Hemispheres, and the moon's apogee and perigee are fixed numbers and tell us how far away it is at any given time. Then there are geographic locations that aren't quite as definite. Neverland is located at the second star to the right and straight on 'til morning. Brigadoon can only be found one day every one hundred years in an enchanted forest, and Oz as we all know is somewhere over the rainbow.

Easy reference map that identifies New York's sixty-two counties. *Wikimedia Commons.*

That brings us to Upstate New York, a vague geographic designation and the focus of this book. For some, Upstate is everything north of the New York metropolitan area and its suburbs, which includes bits of New Jersey and Connecticut. The Department of Environmental Conservation considers Upstate as everything except New York City and Long Island. A more expansive definition set by the U.S. Census Bureau includes Westchester, Rockland and Putnam as downstate. Some use the Metro-North railroad line as an indicator, noting that if that line serves you, you are not Upstate, and still others gauge the distinction by Interstate 84. Look at a map of New York and its sixty-two distinct counties. You'll find that an overwhelming majority are in the area considered by most standards as being Upstate, with some in Rockland, Putnam, Dutchess and Hudson being a bit vaguer. For this book, I've determined anything north of Poughkeepsie as Upstate. Cartographers: we can agree to disagree.

Living in the shadow of the five boroughs can be daunting. Geographically speaking, New York City is not even 1 percent of the state, yet it exerts an influence and pull vastly outsized by its actual footprint. I would be the last person to minimize the culinary contributions of NYC. I am so enamored of its foodways that I wrote a book about its iconic offerings. However, I never fully realized the amazing culinary contributions that have come from the remaining 99 percent of the state. I never considered the terroir that encourages Concord grapes and dry Riesling. I didn't fully appreciate the growers who keep us sated with crisp fall apples and hard cider or the more than one hundred species of fish that swim in its waterways.

In delving into the foods that are the signature of Upstate New York, you first need to be mindful that you cannot sweep the entire portion of the state into one genre. Western New York has nuances different than Central New York, and Central has different styles than the Finger Lakes. Each region's foods reflect its distinct personality, so I apologize in advance when I group the entire portion of Upstate New York into one.

There are some things I need you to accept if we're going to take this journey together. I ask forgiveness for omitting your favorite local food or haunt. It would be impossible to capture every iteration of a dish, so broad strokes were needed to prevent this book from being one thousand pages. I concede that your favorite hangout does have the best version of Buffalo wings, I am sure the tomato pie from your neighborhood bakery is more satisfying and the sponge candy from your confectioner is sweeter. Please excuse the plethora of puns. My pun monitor was udderly overwhelmed in my discussion of dairy cows. And you need to accept the role of food lore in many of the origin stories related to the people who innovated a dish. Food lore, much like folklore, is an accepted mashup of fact and legend. It tends to lend color and context as well as dubious "facts."

The monumental achievements of Upstate New York from the Erie Canal to the Pan-American Exposition paint Upstate in the forward and progressive light it deserves to be seen. It is a region that created an entire genre of vacationing through the abundant food of the Borscht Belt and was home to a legendary music festival held in the summer of 1969. It is a center for higher learning, with a wide range of colleges and universities that have all contributed to the culinary experience. The personality of blue-collar factory towns populated by immigrants informs Upstate against a backdrop of the vibrancy of Saratoga. It's exploring the wine and cheese trails weaving through the Finger Lakes and Hudson Valley and fishing for trout in Central New York. An Upstate exploration is traveling through regions named for Native Americans and honoring the Haudenosaunee at the Ganondagan State Historic Site. It can take you around the globe with its foreign-sounding cities as you enjoy Cuba Cheese in Mexico, grape pie

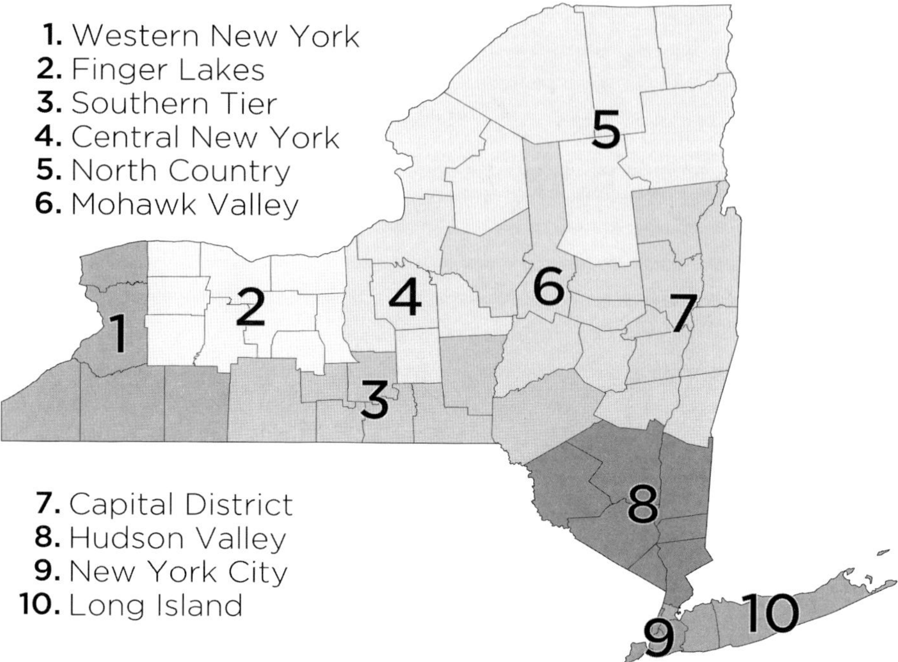

Map identifying the regions of Upstate New York. *Wikimedia Commons.*

in Naples or poutine in Ontario County. It can confuse you with a dish called the garbage plate—purported to cure a hangover—and impress you with a harmoniously balanced black and white cookie in the region where it was truly born. This is an area that improvised, popularized and canonized dishes that you might have never heard of, let alone tasted. It's a road trip well worth taking, albeit not on a snowy winter day. It is an experience that you'll be able to re-create in your home using the recipes presented. This is a journey filled with backcountry roads, less-than-glossy dining rooms and authentic New York accents (no Brooklynese here). It is rebirthing and renewing traditional dishes while sanctifying the classics. And most of all, it's just plain fun, so enjoy the ride.

Chapter 1

THE FIRST NEW YORKERS

The story of Upstate New York's food and culture is a tale of two people. The first is the Indigenous, having been there for hundreds of years. They worshipped the landscape; devoted themselves to cultivating it; and imbued the region with their language, traditions and values. They were a people with roots that were upended as they were displaced and their lifestyle and contributions were absorbed. The second group was in search of a new place rather than clinging to their home. They came with little and created a life in a new land, bringing their traditions with them in tow. One group left much behind while the other brought much forward. They both imprinted on Upstate New York, making indelible contributions to the area. Subsequent chapters highlight the contributions of immigrants, but this first chapter is dedicated to the first people, most specifically the Iroquois, who migrated east from the Bering Strait and settled much of New York. As this book focuses on foodways, I will leave the in-depth historical context to historians, but here is a brief overview to help you appreciate their important place in the foodways of Upstate New

A depiction of the "Passport of the Iroquois League." This signifies them as a sovereign nation; the first was issued in 1923. *Wikimedia Commons, Matthew G. Bisanz.*

A 1913 sketch of an Iroquois longhouse. *Wikimedia Commons. From* Stories in American History *by Wilbur F. Gordy.*

York. The Iroquois, known more appropriately as the Haudenosaunee Confederacy, were farming the Mohawk Valley as far back as the 1600s. The confederacy consisted of five tribes: the Cayuga, Onondaga, Seneca, Oneida and Mohawk. A sixth tribe, the Tuscarora people, joined to form the Six Nations of the Haudenosaunee.

The State of New York recognized the six-tribe nation in 1722, and it was regarded as one of the first true democracies. As wars raged with allegiances stretched between the colonists, British and French, the loyalty of the Indigenous people was splintered. However, in 1784, a treaty signed in Canandaigua, New York, between the United States and the Haudenosaunee cemented the right of each to live peacefully and undisturbed by the other. As Laura Falk wrote in her book *Culinary History of the Finger Lakes*, they were a matriarchal society and women were held in high esteem, holding important roles in both the societal and governmental aspects. They lived in longhouses (and were therefore referred to as "people of the longhouse") and were proficient in hunting, fishing and agricultural pursuits.

The Three Sisters

Their farming skills focused on a trio of crops known as the Three Sisters. This triumvirate of corn, beans and squash was a spiritual and synergistic alliance. They represented a bond between the Haudenosaunee and the land. Dr. Jane Mt. Pleasant, a Cornell University professor of agriculture and a Native American descendant, describes the Three Sisters in detail:

> *The first sister is corn. Corn is the eldest sister. She stands up tall and straight....She is serious, important, and responsible. She is the engine of the trio....The second sister is Bean. Bean is shy and twines herself around the legs of her elder sister....She also provides nitrogen to the other sisters, by converting nitrogen from the air into a form...the plants need to survive. The third sister is Squash....She stays close to the ground, is kind of impish and wild....Squash also provides valuable vitamins, minerals, oils, and protein.*

The Haudenosaunee used the Three Sisters to their fullest potential, creating soups, vegetable medleys, bread and meat-based stews for their well-rounded diets. They were not only accomplished farmers but also proficient hunters and fishermen. To impart sweetness to their food, they added maple syrup. Legend says the syrup was discovered accidentally when a tomahawk tossed into the air landed in a maple tree, creating a serendipitous spigot. The Haudenosaunee Confederacy website wants you to know that they were resourceful people. They enriched soups with tree bark, used the oil from owls as medicine and educated their children in their ways by engaging them to protect seedlings. Their methods were sophisticated and innovative, burning tree trunks to prepare the fields, creating rotations in crews and using elk antlers as hoes.

Of all the food traditions imparted by Native Americans to Europeans, one has garnered new attention through the White Corn Project. White corn, one of the Three Sisters, was integral to the Haudenosaunee. It was very nutritious with a low glycemic index; naturally slow to digest; filling; and rich in nutrients, protein and fiber.

A conceptual drawing of the Three Sisters showing the interdependence of corn, beans and squash. *Wikimedia Commons, Garlan Miles.*

The revitalization of white corn as a coveted crop has become the responsibility of a project housed at the Ganondagan State Historic Site. There they are enlisting Seneca farmers to help cultivate the crop, reestablishing the connection between the Seneca Nation and this food. Ganondagan was the largest village of the Seneca Nation, so it stands to reason that when the late

Dr. John Mohawk (member of the Seneca Nation) and his wife, the late Dr. Yvonne Dion Buffalo (Samson Cree), developed the initiative, they found farmland in the area where the Seneca Nation thrived. Dr. Mohawk prized the food value of Indigenous heritage food. As a food panelist for a group called the Bioneers, he was quoted as saying, "The food value in commercial food is weighed in dollars, and the food value in heritage foods is weighed in something we might call life force." Under the leadership of G. Peter Jemison, the project remains vibrant. They tout sales of over five thousand pounds of corn a year. Jemison noted, "We quickly realized we weren't going to get rich doing this," and rejected offers from major companies to market it, adding, "What they wanted would hurt what we had set out to do, which is bring this back to our people." Since the inception of the project, the Seneca Nation has established a farm where the tribal members reconnect with their roots. This was certainly one of the goals of this initiative. In the "Where to Go" section at the end of the book, details are provided so you can support this mission.

To summarize the skills of Native Americans in the landscape of New York foodways, I'll leave you with this comment by eighteenth-century

An image of a Native American woman and child in the Lake George area preparing food. *NYPL Digital Collections.*

historian James Adair, who was an observer of their practices. We owe them a deep debt of gratitude and the respect they so rightly have earned.

They (the native Americans) are acquainted with a great many herbs and roots, of which the general part of the English has not the least knowledge. If an Indian were driven out into the extensive woods, with only a knife and a tomahawk, or small hatchet, it is not to be doubted but he would fatten, even if a wolf would starve. He could soon start a fire, by rubbing two dry pieces of wood together, make a bark hut, make earthen vessels, and a bow and arrow; then kill wild game, fish, fresh water turtles, gather a plentiful variety of vegetables and live in affluence.

• • • • • • • • • •

Recipe: Succotash

Before writing this book, I thought succotash was either a punch line spoken by Sylvester, a cartoon cat, or a very boring side dish. I now know that it is a vegetable medley that honors the Haudenosaunee. The word derives from a Narragansett Indian word, *msickquatash*, which roughly translates to "broken" or "boiled corn." The dish pays homage to the Three Sisters, pillars of Native American agriculture. You can add or subtract any ingredients you have on hand or prefer not to include, but try to prepare it in the summer months when fresh corn, pole-climbing green beans and vine-ripe tomatoes are available.

Serves 6–8 as a side dish
Start to finish: 1 hour 15 minutes

1 medium spaghetti squash, seeds removed
Olive oil
Kosher salt
2 tablespoons butter
1 small onion, finely chopped
6 ounces fresh green beans, trimmed and cut into ¼-inch pieces
1 small red pepper, cored, seeded and cut into ¼-inch pieces
1 medium-sized zucchini, cut into ¼-inch pieces
2 garlic cloves, minced
3 cups corn kernels (about 3 ears)

1 cup small green or white lima beans, frozen or canned
1 cup quartered grape tomatoes
Freshly cracked black pepper
¼ cup Parmesan cheese

Preheat the oven to 400 degrees.

Cut the spaghetti squash in half, lengthwise, and remove the seeds. You don't want to remove too much flesh, so a knife or kitchen shears can help you release the seeds more easily. Drizzle the squash with a touch of olive oil and a light sprinkling of kosher salt. Place them cut side down on a parchment-lined baking sheet, prick the outer skin with a fork and roast for 30 minutes. While the squash roasts, prep your vegetables.

Heat 2 tablespoons of olive oil and the butter in a skillet. Add the chopped onions and cook, over medium-high heat, for about 5 minutes. Drop in the green beans, red pepper, zucchini and garlic. Cook and stir for about 5 minutes until the vegetables begin to take on a light golden color.

Add the corn, lima beans and tomatoes. Season with about ½ teaspoon of kosher salt and ¼ teaspoon of freshly cracked black pepper. Cook an additional 5 minutes.

While the vegetables cook, use a fork to create the spaghetti strands with your squash; set aside.

Spoon the vegetable mixture into a baking dish. Top with the spaghetti squash, scattering it to cover the entire dish. Drizzle with a touch of olive oil, ½ teaspoon of kosher salt, a few turns of black pepper and the Parmesan cheese. Bake for about 30 minutes or until the top is lightly browned. You can place the dish under the broiler at the end to crisp up even more.

Chapter 2

UPSTATE'S GREATEST HITS

Had David Letterman been familiar with the regional dishes that characterize Upstate New York, he might have renamed his list from the top ten to the lucky thirteen. That's my count of the dishes that most represent the personality of the area. The influences of immigrants are felt in many preparations as the foods were designed to be practical, efficient and reflective of their homeland's cuisine. They are filled with flavor, food lore and fun facts. Best to have plenty of napkins on hand, even when reading about them, as drooling may occur. Just to ensure the mouthwatering effect they deserve, color photos of these foods can be found in the insert of this book.

Beef on Weck

If a French dip roast beef sandwich and cozy slippers had a love child, the result would be beef on weck. This staple of Western New York, most specifically Buffalo, is like slipping into a well-worn booth in your favorite tavern. To the uninitiated, you might wonder, beef on what? The beef part is easy to explain. A slow-roasted rare roast beef is gently hand-carved into paper-thin slices and mounded onto a roll after having been bathed in natural beef juices. It is then topped with prepared horseradish or, for some iconoclasts, horseradish cream. That sounds pretty straightforward, but it's the weck that might be throwing you. Weck is short for kümmelweck (kimmelweck, kummelweck). Its name derives from the Kaiser-style roll that cocoons the mountain of meat. In German, *kummel* means "caraway" and *weck* means "roll," so a kummelweck roll is one coated in pungent caraway seeds with the addition of coarse pretzel-like salt. At one time, Buffalo boasted a large German immigrant population, so much so that one of its oldest churches, Saint Ann's, established by German Roman Catholics, was one of the nation's largest. According to the church's website, their school enrollment topped that of any school, parochial, private or public, in the country. So it was no surprise that a Bavarian-inspired roll brimming with perfectly cooked roast beef would be a hit, even at a whopping fifteen cents! It was also a win for pub owners, who were said to encourage their patrons to order the sandwich as the copious amount of salt made for a thirsty tavern goer and the beers just kept coming. The sandwich was often accompanied by a bowl of flavorful beef juices for those who like to take the plunge and extra prepared or creamy horseradish on the side to add a hefty tang and clear your sinuses. And let's not overlook the kosher dill spear sitting humbly on the side of the plate.

Some credit the Delaware House with serving the first beef on weck, or so says John Guenther, who shared his family's story with What'sCookingAmerica.net. As he related it, his great-grandfather Joe Gohn was the proprietor of the Delaware House, a small saloon, which was conveniently located across the street from one of the entrances to the 1901 Pan-American Exposition. Hungry and thirsty visitors to the exposition embarked and disembarked the trolley, landing them at the doorsteps of the Delaware House. Their German baker created the sandwich to feed the appetites and encourage the thirst of these exposition goers. Standard Oil purchased the Delaware House in 1931, and it was later razed to make way for a gas station. All was not lost, however: Joe opened another tavern named Gohn's, where he continued to serve the sandwich.

This all seems entirely plausible, yet a touch of suspicion is cast by Cheryl Staycheck, the current owner of Schwabl's, a local eatery known for its stupendous beef on weck. Cheryl suspects the sandwich might have originated at their establishment in 1901, and it has remained on their menu ever since. At Schwabl's, the meat is expertly carved by hand and can be ordered anywhere from medium to rare. What makes their beef on weck unique? You might have asked the late Anthony Bourdain, who visited the restaurant on a wintry January day back in 2009. The reason for his visit is as interesting as the visit itself. Local musician Nelson Starr entered a contest in which the prize was a visit to your community by Bourdain. As reported in the *Buffalo News*, although Starr was the runner-up, he convinced Bourdain to come to Buffalo as part of his Rust Belt episode. Bourdain was enamored with Schwabl's beef on weck, declaring it to be "a tasty little masterpiece." Not bad from a food aficionado who dined with Francis Ford Coppola at a palace once owned by Mussolini and slurped noodles with President Barack Obama in a Hanoi joint. If you become obsessed with this beloved sandwich, you're not alone; there's a Facebook group of over seventeen thousand who call themselves the Beef on Weck Appreciation Society. Your membership is pending.

The caraway seed is actually the dried fruit of the caraway plant. It has a pungent flavor and is often used in German cooking and baking. *Unsplash, Katrina Wright.*

• • • • • • • • • •

Recipe: Beef on Weck

You can recreate this mouthwatering Upstate sandwich easily at home. Feel free to take a shortcut and buy thinly sliced rare deli roast beef and a horseradish dressing. To make an authentic sandwich, don't skip preparing a homemade kummelweck roll; that's what elevates beef on weck from a traditional roast beef sandwich.

Serves 6 people
Start to finish: 1½–2 hours

1 (3-pound) eye round
Kosher salt and fresh cracked black pepper
2 garlic cloves, cut into lengthwise slivers
1 cup beef broth

Let the beef come to room temperature 1 hour before roasting.

Preheat the oven to 450 degrees.

Generously season the beef with kosher salt and pepper to create a flavorful crust. Cut small slits throughout the top of the roast and insert the garlic slivers.

Roast for 15 minutes at 450, reduce temp to 350 and roast until medium rare, about 45 minutes longer.

Or 2 pounds thinly sliced rare deli roast beef (you'll need to buy a packet of gravy to prepare the jus)

Kummelweck Roll

6 Kaiser rolls
1 egg white, beaten
½ teaspoon caraway seeds
1 teaspoon kosher salt

Preheat the oven to 300 degrees. Brush the top of the rolls with the egg white and sprinkle ¼ teaspoon of caraway seeds (more if you like a pungent roll) and a scant ¼ teaspoon of salt on each. Bake for 5–8 minutes until the tops have browned slightly. Remove from the oven and slice each roll in half.

Horseradish Cream

¼ cup mayo
¼ cup sour cream
3 tablespoons prepared horseradish
Kosher salt and pepper to taste

Mix all ingredients in a small bowl and chill until ready to use.

Assembly

Heat the jus in a medium saucepan. Remove the horseradish cream from the fridge, and cut the rolls in half. Dip the sliced beef in the jus to warm up a bit but be sure you do not overcook it; you want the beef to remain rare. Pile the beef on the roll. Dip the top half of the roll in the jus and then spread horseradish cream on top. Close the sandwich and serve with a dipping bowl of jus on the side and a dill pickle spear.

Buffalo Wings

Hold on to your hot sauce, we have hit on the OG of Upstate food, the bar bite and football-frenzied food that put Buffalo, New York, on the culinary map. There is very little dispute that the recipe of Buffalo wings as we know them today originated in Buffalo. Simply put, a wing that is fried and bathed in a spicy sauce was inarguably a Buffalo invention. And for once, we can pinpoint the first to prepare them.

Like so many food discoveries, the Buffalo wing was born out of ingenuity. Teresa Bellissimo, along with her husband, Frank, owned the Anchor Bar in Buffalo, New York. On March 4, 1964, Teresa faced a late-night crowd composed of mostly her son Dominic's friends. Needing something quick to cook up to feed the crowd, Teresa reached for the wings that she usually added to the pot when making stock. She separated them at the joint, fried them up, doused them in hot sauce and served them gratis to these late-night barflies. The frugal chef then added celery from their antipasto platter and bleu cheese dressing from their house salad, and voilà, a star was born. 99.9 percent of grateful wing lovers accept this story as fact. But it wouldn't be a food story without another version. Enter John Young, who claims ownership of the Buffalo wing. His sauce, which he called "mombo," covered the wings he prepared at his restaurant, Wings N' Things, on Jefferson Avenue in Buffalo. Residents remember chowing down on Young's wings about the same time Anchor Bar developed its reputation for having invented them. A colorful local mural features the city of Buffalo and proclaims John Young "The King of Wings." It was funded by a GoFundMe campaign and donations from area organizations.

Buffalonians devour copious amounts of chicken wings, as attested by the city's proclamation in 1977 that July 29 be forever deemed Chicken Wing Day. The proclamation goes on to sanctify the day as "thousands of pounds

If you want to be simply authentic, then Frank's is the way to go. *Unsplash, dischatz.*

of chicken wings are consumed by Buffalonians in restaurants and taverns throughout the city each week." In 2017, the National Chicken Council estimated that Americans will eat 1.33 billion chicken wings on Super Bowl Sunday. According to the NCC, that's enough wings to circle the earth three times. In a truly fun fact, they estimate that if an NFL player ate 2 wings per minute, it would take him 1,265 years, 80 days, 7 hours and 12 minutes to eat 1.33 billion wings. The National Chicken Council reports that Dick Winger (yes, that is his real last name), who sold the hot sauce to the Bellissimos, went on the road with Dominic promoting the wings to restaurants across the country. Wings soon became associated with sporting events as bars realized they could prepare and serve this delicious pickup food for very little money and reap the additional reward of wing lovers lingering at the bar, watching the game and ordering beers to wash them down.

It's no surprise that the national fast-food chain Buffalo Wild Wings was started by Buffalo natives as an homage to their favorite food. They have since sold to another food chain, but they were in part responsible for preaching the gospel of the Buffalo-style wing to the uninitiated. This humble food has spread its global wings as honey mustard, sweet chili and BBQ versions have become ubiquitous. But if you're craving the original, opt for a simple dunk of butter mixed with Frank's hot sauce.

CHICKEN RIGGIES

There is a Utica, New York specialty where every ingredient elevates the next. It is a combination of chicken, hot peppers and a flavorful tomato-based cream sauce all tossed with rigatoni pasta, hence the nickname *riggies* (pronounced with a soft *g*). This decidedly Italian American creation is surprisingly nuanced, with the balance of hot, vinegary peppers that permeate every bite and play off the sweet velvety sauce, which originally came from lots of grated cheese that was blended with chicken stock and white wine. The chicken is simply along for the ride. It is satisfying and available in just about every Italian restaurant in Oneida County. The Italian community has made an impact in that county since the arrival of what is reported to be the first immigrant of Italian descent to settle there in 1817. According to the Ethnic Heritage Studies Center at Utica University, Dr. John B. Marchisi was a prosperous pharmacist and the first of thousands to arrive during the great migration between 1880 and 1920. Many of the arrivals found work as laborers, while some were entrepreneurial and ran small businesses. Italian-language newspapers sprang up, and Oneida County reflected the rich culture of these newcomers. By the early 1900s, the Italian community had become a political force, with some scholars crediting this voting block for igniting FDR's run for governor in 1928. These immigrants brought with them foodways from their homeland, which infused and informed the dishes that Utica residents would come to call their own. Chicken riggies is perhaps the best example of that integration of the old world into the new. According to Bill Keeler of WIBX, Utica's news radio, the original dish might not have been first made in Utica but rather was made famous there. It seems that the dish was conceived in nearby Clinton, at the Clinton House. Keeler spoke with the late great area chef Michael Geno, who vividly recalls that he was there the first time the dish was dished out. Monday nights, according to Geno, attracted a group of doctors, lawyers and "union guys who would come in on Monday nights to play cards." He says they made for them "the riggie dish with chicken, tomatoes, and cherry peppers." This became a weekly habit, and the legacy of chicken riggies was affirmed.

Several other area chefs have a different recollection. Mike Schulz, who was a dishwasher at the Clinton House in the 1970s, says it was a dish they whipped up to feed the kitchen staff. When Schulz left the Clinton House and became a chef at Chesterfield Restaurant, he added chicken

Nothing but rigatoni can be used in this iconic Italian dish. *Wikimedia Commons, Popo de Chien.*

riggies to the menu, and as he says, "The rest is history." Not taking credit for conceiving the dish, Schulz does feel his adding it to the menu is what established it as a classic. Not to be left out of the conversation, enter Jeff Daniels, whose father owned Café Daniele's on James and Mohawk Streets. He cites a similar dish on their menu that they called "chicken caprice." He recalls his dad serving their version over rigatoni pasta and said, "That's how we believe the dish started." Perhaps the final word should go to the late chef Joe Morelle. He recalled the dish being served at Anthony's, also on Mohawk Street. In a true game of telephone, he knew a guy who knew a guy who knew a guy named Joey Pristera, who originated the dish. He also credited Grimaldi's on Bleeker, as so many of the chefs involved in the mystery of chicken riggies got their start there. Whoever created it and wherever it started, the good news is that chicken riggies is still a local favorite and everyone has now put their spin on it.

• • • • • • • • •

Recipe: Chicken Riggies

Do your mouth a flavor and make this next time you want something nourishing and nurturing, designed to feed a crowd. There are many versions of chicken riggies, but I didn't want to stray too far from the original. You can make it your own by adjusting the heat level and type of chicken you use, but please, don't use any pasta other than rigatoni; it would be blasphemy.

Serves: 6–8
Start to finish: About 30 minutes

2–3 tablespoons olive oil
2 pounds boneless, skinless chicken breasts cut into 1-inch pieces or the equivalent of chicken thighs
2 teaspoons kosher salt
¼ teaspoon black pepper
1 pound rigatoni (Mezzi Rigatoni no. 26)
½ cup (about half a 10-ounce jar) roasted red peppers, chopped
¼ cup (about 3–4) mild heat pepperoncini, seeded and chopped
½ cup (about 6–8) sweet cherry peppers, seeded and chopped (for more heat, use hot peppers)
¼ cup sundried tomatoes, chopped
2 tablespoons chopped garlic from about 3–5 cloves
½ cup dry white wine
½ cup chicken broth
1 can whole plum San Marzano tomatoes
½ cup grated pecorino Romano cheese
½ cup half-and-half or light cream

Bring a large pot of salted water to boil.

Heat 2 tablespoons olive oil in a large, deep skillet. When shimmering hot, add the chicken. Season with 1 teaspoon of salt and the black pepper. Cook over medium-high heat until the bottoms are lightly brown, about 4 minutes; turn and cook an additional 3–4 minutes. Using a slotted spoon, remove the chicken pieces and place them in a bowl; cover and set aside.

In the same pan, add the remaining teaspoon of oil, the chopped roasted peppers, pepperoncini, cherry peppers, sundried tomatoes and chopped garlic. Cook for about 2 minutes. Add the wine and broth, scraping any bits from the bottom of the pan. Cook over medium-high heat for about 2 minutes.

Begin cooking your pasta.

To the skillet add the whole tomatoes, crushing them in your hands over the skillet to release the juices. Season with the remaining 1 teaspoon of kosher salt. Cook over medium-low heat about 5 minutes. Add the chicken and stir to coat all the pieces. Cover and cook so the chicken cooks all the way through.

Drain the pasta, reserving ½ cup pasta water. Add the pasta, cheese, cream and ¼ cup pasta water to the skillet and stir to combine. Add additional pasta water to achieve the sauce level you prefer. Serve right from the skillet, with an extra dusting of grated cheese and a sprinkling of red pepper flakes for added heat, if desired.

GARBAGE PLATE

The kitchen sink is a greasy spoon menu staple. The item is generally a conglomeration of multiple food elements that loosely go together and complete the phrase: this contains everything but… Much the same can be said of a Rochester concoction that throws together more disparate ingredients than should ever appear on the same plate. Unlike the kitchen sink, which often makes sense, this dish is truly a hodgepodge of individually tasty foods that when they come together should make your head explode. However, according to those in the know, mainly college students in this college-driven town, it has the complete opposite effect. Instead of causing an explosion, it is said to relieve a headache, make the morning after a frat party bearable and allow one to face the day hangover-free. I'm talking about the garbage plate, a receptacle of mismatched foods that came together in one of Rochester's greatest culinary achievements.

What exactly comprises this dish with the off-putting name? It is a mashup of hamburger (or cheeseburger), hotdogs locally known as white or red hots,

Italian sausage, chicken or possibly grilled cheese served on top of any or all of the following: French fries, home fries, baked beans and, wait for it, macaroni salad. But that's not all. The plate is topped with mustard, onions and a meat sauce that's one part hot sauce and another part oily ragu. And if that wasn't enough, a side of thick-cut white bread accompanies the dish. And yes, this is a dish to prevent you from sharing what you ate the day before, not encourage it.

It all began with Alexander Tahou, a Greek immigrant who opened a restaurant in 1918, calling the establishment West Main Texas Hots. Alex, the founder's grandson, notes that it was a plate designed to feed a hungry diner for a low cost. It appealed to the immigrant community, both Greek and German, as the hots featured in the dish came from the venerable sausage maker Zweigle's, which has been grinding out meat in Rochester since 1880. At the start, the dish was called hots and potatoes—that was before college students swarmed the restaurant and asked for a plate with all that garbage on it. Alex told me that they didn't mind when students asked for all the garbage to be thrown in but did take exception to it then being called the garbage plate, which impugned the ingredients. That all changed in 1992, when Tahou embraced the colloquial term and registered a trademark with the U.S. Patent and Trademark Office. The labeling reads that a garbage plate is "prepared entrees consisting primarily of one of the following, hotdogs without buns, hamburgers without buns, steak, pork chops, sausage, ham, fish, or eggs and processed potatoes and processed beans." Many have imitated the dish, but none can call it a garbage plate. You know a dish has a legion of loyal followers when the home team, the Rochester Red Wings, celebrates it at a home game. The night they celebrated the dish's one hundredth anniversary, the players wore uniforms with illustrations of the layers of the dish and concession stands featured themed offerings. The team general manager noted, "As a community, we take immense pride in things that are unique to our town." The garbage plate ranks very high on that list. Perhaps Meghan O'Dea, in her piece on the garbage plate for Eater.com, said it best: "Like Rochester itself, the garbage plate has a little bit of everything. Anywhere else this would be a disorganized mess, a picnic gone awry, a child chef's attempt at alchemy. In Rochester, it's home."

While the exact dish is often served only in Rochester, its fame or infamy was shared across the country as comedian Jim Gaffigan riffed on the dish after sampling a plate before a concert in Upstate New York. In an interview with Conan O'Brien, he discussed his experience at Tahou's and the garbage plate, calling it delicious and noting the weird combination of cold and hot ingredients was unique and confusing. He said that he had still not recovered, noting that Rochester, Minnesota, is noted for its hospital and healing and that its sister city, Rochester, New York, is noted for food that could kill you. Gaffigan remarked, "There's obviously no health department in Rochester." Not so fast to judge, countered Dr. Mike Mendoza, who represents the health department. He noted they had more important issues, busy dealing with the pandemic. He invited Gaffigan to sample a garbage plate with him "when this is all over." Subsequently, Gaffigan posted a YouTube video showing his family at home enjoying the garbage plate, courtesy of the restaurant; he even sported a Nick Tahou T-shirt.

To get a true grip on the garbage plate, I made a trip to Rochester and spoke to the source, Alex Tahou, grandson of the original owner and son of Nick, who renamed the place Nick Tahou Hots. I also shared a garbage plate with my husband. I can't say I was enamored of the experience, but I will say the ingredients were all really good on their own, well-cooked burgers, dogs with a bite, creamy macaroni salad and perfectly crisp fries. Just questioning our judgment to eat this before getting into the car for a four-hour journey home. Suffice it to say, we made it with minutes to spare

If you want the original, then there's only one place to go—Nick Tahou Hots. *Courtesy of Nick Tahou.*

and a promise to go back and do it all over again on our next road trip. It was surprisingly addictive. To re-create this dish at home, I suggest you gather up your various leftovers from your last Fourth of July family cookout and a plate of spaghetti Bolognese and do Rochester a solid by piling this mashup of food on your plate, hangover optional.

Grape Pie

Welcome to the 2020s, when the term *grape pie* can mean two very different things. To Upstate New Yorkers, it is a deeply satisfying, not cloyingly sweet fruit pie. It was popularized in Naples, New York, in the mid-1900s by Irene Bouchard, who has since been dubbed the grape pie queen. However, if you google "grape pie," you might get an interesting hit, and I use that term literally. Grape pie is also the name, according to askgrowers.com, of a type of marijuana described as "the child strain of highly potent parents—Cherry Pie and Grape Stomper. It can make one giggly, euphoric, and happy." What a coincidence—so does the original grape pie, where Concord grapes are baked into a buttery crust with a bit of sugar and no psychoactive compounds.

For this book, we'll focus on the dessert grape pie, not the compound that could create a scenario where you crave grape pie. Like so many foods that originate in and are particular to a certain region, grape pie was born out of the abundance of sweet Concord grapes available in the Finger Lakes region at the height of fall's fruit season. Naples sits at the south end of Canandaigua Lake. It's a small town where the grapes outnumber the residents. In Naples, grape pie ranks right up there with apple and pumpkin as an autumn treat and is relatively simple in form. The flavor of grape pie is a hybrid, like its cannabis doppelganger, but one that blends the sweet taste of Manischewitz wine with the consistency of grape jelly. It has a surprising mouthfeel, as the peels from the grapes play an integral part in the preparation.

Grape pie is made from a type of grape called a slip-skin. That essentially means that to extract the pulp, you needn't peel the grapes, you simply coax them out of their skins with a pinch and a push. The pulp is then boiled down with sugar and a thickener, much like a jam, and then the skins are added back in to create a unique texture and sweet tart balance of flavor. This is a "don't knock it till you've tried it" pie. According to Jennifer Morrisey,

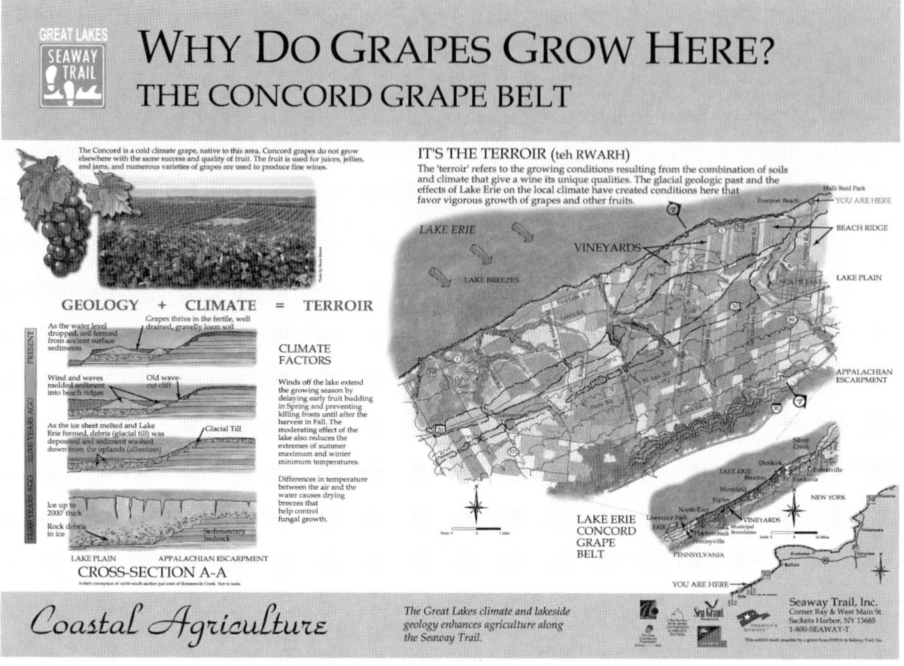

The grape belt stretches from western New York to Pennsylvania; it's all about the terroir. *Wikimedia Commons, Great Lakes Seaway Trail.*

who in 2016 wrote about this typical Naples dessert, the owner of the local Redwood Restaurant wanted a new and novel dessert to feed his guests. In the early 1960s, he added Bouchard's pie to his fall menu.

Making the pie can be a laborious task. Craig "Meathead" Goldwyn, author of the bestselling book *The Science of Great Barbecue and Grilling*, had the opportunity to meet with Irene before she passed almost a decade ago to observe her pie-baking prowess. Goldwyn reported Bouchard baked about eighteen thousand pies a year, six thousand grape pies in the fall and twelve thousand other varieties in the remaining months. He recalled that she would "preheat her two regular kitchen ovens at 2:30 am when the lake air cooled her kitchen and not quit until 4:30 pm baking four pies at a time in each oven." Irene's dutiful husband, Don, was said to have skinned two and a half tons of grapes, taking his marriage vows to a new level.

• • • • • • • • •

Recipe: Concord Grape Tart

For those who know the dubious pleasure of sipping Manischewitz wine or the childlike joy of drinking a cup of grape juice, Concord grape pie is a must-try. The grapes have a sweet yet tart bite; pop one in your mouth and it creates a subtle grapey sensation that is intoxicating. Take those same grapes and turn them into jelly, a pie or a sandwich cookie, and you are in for a treat. This tart is a riff on grape pie, sans the double crust. I've included a recipe for streusel topping if you want to take it up a notch.

Makes: 1 pie
Start to finish: About 3 hours (20 minutes hands on, 3 hours for ingredients to chill/bake)

Filling

4 cups (about 24 ounces) Concord grapes
½ cup granulated white sugar
2 tablespoons cornstarch

Crust

2 cups all-purpose flour
1 pinch kosher salt
3 tablespoons granulated white sugar
1 cup (2 sticks) cold unsalted butter, cut into small cubes
2 tablespoons white vinegar

Streusel Topping (Optional)

½ cup all-purpose flour
¼ cup brown sugar (light or dark)
¼ cup rolled oats
1 pinch kosher salt
½ teaspoon ground cinnamon
4 tablespoons room-temperature butter

Rinse the grapes and remove the stems. Pinch the grapes at one end and pop them out of their skins and into a small saucepan. Reserve the skins. Heat on medium, mashing them down a bit for about 7–10 minutes until they are very mushy and have released their juices. Strain the grapes over a bowl, pressing out the flesh and juice; discard the seeds.

Wipe out the saucepan and return the grapes to the pot, adding the skins, sugar and cornstarch. Stir to combine and heat on medium heat until the mixture thickens, about 7–10 minutes, stirring every few minutes to help break down the skins. Pour the mixture into a bowl, and when it comes to room temperature, cover and refrigerate until completely chilled, at least 2 hours.

When the grapes are chilled, prepare the dough. Combine the flour, salt and sugar in the bowl of a food processor fitted with a metal blade. Pulse to combine. Add the butter to the bowl and pulse until the mixture forms a crumb-like consistency. Bits of butter should still be visible. Drizzle in the vinegar and pulse until a dough forms.

Remove from the bowl and press the dough into a 9-inch tart pan with a removable bottom. The crust should be about ¼ inch thick on the bottom. Press the dough up the sides and trim to remove excess. Refrigerate the crust while you preheat the oven. If using a streusel topping, combine all the ingredients in a bowl and work the butter through with your fingers. The texture should be like pebbles; break up any large clumps.

Fill the shell with the grape mixture and bake at 400 degrees for 1 hour on the lowest rack in the oven. If using the streusel oat topping, scatter the topping over the tart and bake as directed above. Chill before serving (a sprinkle of confectioner's sugar if the tart has no streusel adds a nice touch).

Half Moon Cookies

I am about to blow your cookie-loving mind and shatter a misconception that has been perpetuated for more than a century. The beloved cookie with its harmonious frosting, cake-like texture and ubiquitous presence commonly known as the black and white cookie is not a Jewish bakery delight. That's not to say that Jewish bakers across New York City in the early 1900s didn't turn out thousands of these cookies, displaying them proudly in their front windows. But unlike some other Jewish immigrant–driven culinary creations, the black and white was not born in New York City. It is proudly the invention of Hemstrought's Bakery in Utica, New York. At the time of their first appearances in America, half moon cookies, a.k.a. black and whites and harlequins, were not a unique concept. Bakeries across the country at the turn of the century were dabbling in cakes and cookies that featured contrasting color combinations. Whether decorated with a fluffy frosting or a fondant style, they were a newfangled invention and took the country by storm. You might recall the iconic *Seinfeld* episode where Elaine and Jerry wax poetic about the black and white cookie. It is the seventy-seventh episode of the sixth season in which Jerry and Elaine wander into a NYC bakery to buy dessert for "The Dinner Party" they are attending. Lamenting over the chocolate babka, which had sold out, Jerry is transfixed by the black and white cookies. He theorizes, "The thing about eating a black and white cookie, Elaine, is you want to get some black and some white in each bite. Nothing mixes better than vanilla and chocolate and yet somehow racial harmony eludes us. If people would only look to the cookie all our problems would be solved."

The unity cookie has its roots in Upstate New York, not NYC's Lower East Side. *Author photo.*

Even President Obama got in on the craze when he called the half moon creation "the unity cookie." So, what exactly is a half moon cookie and how does it differ from a black and white? A half moon is a cross between a cookie and a drop cake but favors a cake-like texture more than a black and white. The frosting is a thick layer of chocolate or vanilla whipped buttercream, whereas black and whites downstate usually have a shiny fondant-style frosting. Most likely, Hemstrought's had no idea in 1920 that the cookie they devised would become a staple in every supermarket and bodega from here to its original home of Germany. But make no mistake, America's love affair with this yin-yang confection has its roots in Upstate New York.

The Original Hamburger

There are moments in history that are well-chronicled and definitive. We know when the first human took a step on the moon and when Queen Elizabeth's seventy-year reign came to an end. I wish the same could definitely be said for the invention of America's sandwich, the hamburger. Andrew F. Smith, who wrote the book on the hamburger, explained to me, "Who really invented the hamburger sandwich—strictly defined as a hot ground beef patty served between two pieces of bread—is probably unknowable, but what is clear is that this invention arrived late in the nineteenth century—long after the invention of the sandwich and the ground beef patty." What Smith didn't identify is the where. There seems to be a consensus that this miraculous culinary discovery occurred in Hamburg, New York, just south of Buffalo, in Erie County. It is home to the Erie County Fair, held every August/September since 1868. The Erie County Agricultural Society, which hosts the fair, boasts it was the birthplace of the hamburger, and accounts from most burger aficionados would agree.

Local legend has it that on September 18 at the annual county fair in 1885, Frank and Charles Menches of Canton, Ohio, invented the hamburger as we know it today. The brothers were food vendors at the fair, and the story goes that when they ran out of pork for their signature sandwich, their local meat supplier, Andrew Klein, suggested they substitute ground beef. Upon tasting the cooked ground beef, the Menches brothers added coffee, brown sugar and other ingredients to perk up the flavor and add an unctuous quality. It's said they served it simply with ketchup and sliced onions and named it in honor of the city where the fair was held, Hamburg. Hence, the hamburger was born. It certainly sounds plausible and has added a cachet to the city and annual fair.

Food lore tells us the hamburger has the Erie County Fair to thank for its creation. *Wikimedia Commons, Martybiniasz.*

Not willing to leave well enough alone, Upstate New Yorkers have added their twists to the burger and claim proprietary status to some of their concoctions. One such would be the Bo burger, named for Bo Robertson, who graduated from Cornell in 1958 and was both an Olympic medaling athlete and a pro football player. A burger named for Bo emerged in Ithaca, and it features a hamburger topped with a fried egg and cheese, often with fried or sauteed onions on top. Tracing its roots is as messy as eating a Bo burger, but both are worth the investigation. Some pinpoint the origin to Louie's Lunch on the grounds of Cornell University, while others swear it was Obie's Diner. Whichever eatery can claim ownership is up for debate, but you can still sample a Bo burger at most Ithaca diners and burger joints. There you can also enjoy a Tully burger, which some feel was the precursor to the Big Mac. Peggy Haine of Ithaca.com traced the origins of this cheeseburger topped with raw onion, lettuce, tomato and mayo to Ithaca in the late 1940s–early 1950s. She reported that Cornell historian Corey Earle cited a college hangout known as Wes and Les' that featured this burger, possibly named for a student who dined there named John Martin Tully. A member of Cornell's student body circa 1947 reported that the chef was known to accommodate burger requests, and that's how and when the Tully burger was created. By 1951, the diner was billing itself as "The Home of the Tully Burger," not to be confused with the Whopper, and it could be enjoyed for a whopping twenty-five cents. Ironically, in a town named Tully, they make a Tully burger, albeit those in the know say it is not as authentic. While these creations can certainly be enjoyed in many spots across the country (and at drive-thru windows at major burger chains), Upstate New York stakes a claim to the burger and its tasty iterations. Take that, McDonald's.

HOT DIGGITY DOG

Upstate New York joins the ranks of regions that have hotdog specialties. Some were invented there, others just popularized, but they make Upstate a destination for those hankering for good old-fashioned ballpark food that breaks some of the rules. Prepare to be confused. In the state of Michigan, they eat a hotdog called a Coney dog. In Plattsburgh, New York, they eat a version of that same hotdog, and they call it a Michigan (sometimes spelled with a lowercase *m*). In 1927, Eula and Garth Otis opened a hotdog stand in Plattsburgh serving a hotdog that was a riff on what they ate as residents of Detroit, Michigan. Food lore tells us that Mrs. Otis wanted to pay homage to the state where she and her husband met, so they named the dog a Michigan. The North Country version takes its spices from its Greek heritage with cumin and, in some recipes, cinnamon or allspice. On AdirondackLife.com, Niki Kourofsky gave the Michigan a full rundown. The sauce is thick, filled with ground meat (always started raw in the sauce, never browned first), and has no beans. It gets a kick from a variety of spices, while a squeeze of yellow mustard adds a vinegary zing and coarsely chopped onions create the perfect crunchy bite. You can use any hotdog you choose, but there is a local favorite called the red-skinned hotdog from Glazier's in Malone, New York. Their family has been producing this brand since 1923, so it is entirely plausible that they were the purveyors who supplied the Otis stand. The term *red hot* does not indicate its spice level but rather the very red color of the dog. As for the bun, that's specific as well. No side slide here: the dog is nestled into a steamed top sliced bun, with a composition substantial enough to hold the fully loaded hotdog. When ordering, use local lingo that will make you feel like an insider. Ask for it "buried," which Kourofsky indicates is code for onions tucked under the sauce. If you're craving one now, maybe wait until July, designated in 2021 as "Michigan Month." At that time, Plattsburgh offers Michigan passports. If you have stamps from the four most popular spots that serve this regional version, you get a free T-shirt. As if you needed more incentive to eat four of these dogs.

What do you call a hotdog found in the Capital Region that is teeny, tiny? If you are a creative wordsmith, you might call them wee wieners or bitsy bites. But if you just want to go for the obvious, how about a mini hotdog? Don't let the diminutive name deter you from taking a bite, as it's packed with all the fixings of a Michigan but in a smaller package. Much like a Michigan, there is a Greek history behind these dogs. They were brought to the area by a Greek immigrant, Strates Fentekes, who, according to Albany.com, opened a

Charlie's son John masters the art of the hairy arm. *Courtesy of the Fentekes family.*

restaurant originally called New Way Lunch. The spot became known affectionally as Hot Dog Charlies; as his granddaughter told me, Strates translates to Charlie in English. Fentekes perfected the technique known bluntly as the hairy arm, as he could line up a dozen buns the length of his arm, pop the four-inch dogs in and cover them with the spicy Greek meat sauce, onions and mustard. For you germaphobes, that practice is no longer in effect, so you can leave your hand sanitizer at home. The mini dog has quite a big history. It's been reported that several dozen mini dogs made their way to Moscow in 1958 to be served to the American ambassador to Russia in honor of his fifty-fourth birthday. The restaurant once known as Quick Lunch and now called Famous Lunch was responsible for that shipment and still serves these little treasures today.

There's one more version called the white hot that feels at home Upstate. They differ in size from the mini and in condiments from the Michigan, as spicy brown mustard is the choice to be slathered on the bun. White hots can be likened to bratwurst, as they have a pale color and are packed in a natural casing. They are a combination of pork, beef and veal, and because they are not smoked or cured, they retain the white color. Just as there is more than one top dog Upstate, there's more than one butcher we can credit with bringing this German sausage to the area. It's a shared credit between Rochester's Zweigle and Syracuse's Hoffmann. For Rochester residents, the go-to for their white hot would have to be Zweigels, since 1880, when C. Wilhelm and Josephine Zweigle opened their butcher shop. Zweigels features their trademarked Pop Open hotdog, which is so named as the natural casing shrinks while cooking and the frank pops open. Hoffmann's has them beat by one year, opening in Syracuse in 1879. Both purveyors are multigenerational and still offer their white hots, brats, frankfurters and every iteration of sausage you can name.

Pizza

Upstaters do enjoy a slice of New York–style pizza, which drips with oil and has a foldable crust and a tip that points south just at the precise moment it meets your mouth, but they also put a twist on this classic. You have upside-down pizza, tomato pie, a rolled and fried version with a politically incorrect name and cup and char pepperoni. I am not saying that Upstate New York was the first to create any of these pies, although some might argue they did, but they popularized them and have become known for them, so in this book that counts for a lot.

In paying homage to Upstate's pizza tradition, let's start with O'Scugnizzo's, which is the oldest pizzeria in Upstate New York and the second-oldest continually family-run pizzeria in the country. This Utica landmark is known for its "upside down" pizza, which buries the mozzarella under ladlefuls of intensely flavored tomato sauce. If you are questioning the process, I suggest you first taste the pizza and then consider this: they've been doing it that way since Eugeno Burlino founded the pizzeria in 1914. When we visited the spot, Jessica Burline (the family changed the name's spelling) slid into my booth and shared her family's story. She told me how the name of the pizzeria came to be when her great-grandfather Eugeno started the business. In Italian, *scugnizzo* means "street peddler."

Just look for this sign to taste the best version of upside-down pizza. *Author photo.*

She recalls hearing stories of those in his village calling "hey scugnizzo" when her great-grandfather was peddling his tomato pie on the streets of Naples—hence the name. The genius of this preparation is the cheese is present in every bite, as it is thinly sliced and piled on the thick dough and then the sauce smothers the cheese, a recipe handed down from her great-grandmother. Jessica says that diners often complain that they ordered a pepperoni or sausage pie and don't see either when their pizza comes to the table. That's because they are gently hidden below the cheese and sauce, revealing a delicious surprise with every bite.

Upstaters also enjoy tomato pie, a type of cold or room-temperature pizza distinguished for its chewy crust, lots of tomato sauce and grated cheese, baked in a rectangular pan. It is widely agreed that tomato pie first appeared in Philadelphia, with a focaccia-like dough familiar to Italian immigrants who emigrated from southern Italy to South Philly. Rather than smothering the pie in mozzarella, the pizza gets a dusting of grated "shake" cheese. The pie's fame traveled through New Jersey and Long Island, where it became known as Grandma Pizza, and found a home in Utica. One of the interesting hallmarks of an authentic tomato pie is you don't go to your local pizzeria for a slice. Instead, you head straight to an Italian bakery, where the pie is scored and served much like a coffee cake. I sampled mine at Roma's, which is known for tomato pie. I can attest that their sauce is killer, and the crunch from the crust is audible. When you go, be sure you don't mind eating standing up, as this takeout-only spot has customers tailgating rather than dining.

We now walk a fine line as we keep this book's PG rating and cautiously invoke the term *fat bag*. For some, that denotes a bargain shopper's tote stuffed to the brim. For others, it is an R-rated term that has no place in this chapter. But for those who have ever spent more than five minutes in Canton, New York, it is a pizza that is rolled, hence its alternate and less controversial name "rolled pizza." Once rolled, this usually pepperoni-laden cheesy pocket of dough is then deep-fried. Eating one is like knowingly boarding a sinking ship and then throwing the life preservers in the trash. Think Totino's pizza rolls meet Hot Pockets, and you get the idea. There's a pretty strong consensus that if you are in search of a fat bag, and please don't call it that once you walk through the door, head to Sergi's in Canton, where you can get your fill and then some of their "famous pizza rolls." For the true college town experience, stop by somewhere around 2:00 a.m., order a pizza roll and savor the deep-fried goodness, stringy mozzarella rope and oozing tomato sauce that defines this very Upstate-styled pizza.

Since we're celebrating Upstate pizza uniqueness, let's head to Buffalo, where nary a wing is in sight. Instead, little ringlets of pepperoni are the stars of the show. Here, you'll find cup and char pizza, so named because the edges of the pepperoni curl up just so that they develop a charred crisp, and the centers are like little cups that cradle the spicy meat juices and puddling oil. Insiders call them "roni" cups, and there's a science to the phenomenon that creates the cup and char. The natural casings used to create pepperoni succumb to the heat, causing the casings to curl, rather than laying flat and playing dead in the oven. Battistoni Italian Specialty Meats, which is based in Buffalo, produces the same type they made in 1931 and provides "cup and char" pepperoni to pizza lovers across the country.

It all starts with the dough and a roaring wood fired pizza oven. *Unsplash, Guilherme Maggi.*

Salt Potatoes

Do you know someone who has absolutely no ability in the kitchen and was told they couldn't boil water without a recipe? If so, salt potatoes, a delicious Syracuse born and bred food specialty, are meant for them. In the simplest terms, salt potatoes is a dish composed of the two ingredients mentioned in the name. Salt potatoes were created out of the simple premise of using what you got. Central New Yorkers, specifically those in the Syracuse region on the shores of Onondaga Lake, did just that.

Salt has been a valuable commodity since the beginning of time. As most salt deposits are buried deep beneath the ground, its scarcity made it precious. It carries weight of biblical proportions as Lot's wife can attest. Syracuse was a chief supplier of this mineral, tapping into salt reserves that were created more than 400 million years ago.

This salt formation extended from the Hudson Valley as far as Lake Huron and ran straight through Central New York. So central was salt to this region that Syracuse was once known as the "Salt City." It's no surprise that the canal was sometimes referred to as the "ditch that salt built."

Construction of the Erie Canal, dug by the labor of a large number of Irish immigrants, led to the unique tuber preparation known as salt potatoes. It's no surprise that workers of Irish descent had a familiarity with and affinity for potatoes. Often it was the sole food found in their lunch pail. Their ingenuity led to the creation of salt potatoes, where an abundant resource and an inexpensive ingredient came together. Thin-skinned spring potatoes are boiled in the briny water from the salt springs and produce a potato that has a crusty skin and a creamy center. It boils down to chemistry and physics. The salty water allows the potatoes to come to a boil faster, creating the signature crust. At the higher boiling point, the starchy vegetable cooks more completely to a delectable almost mashed potato texture.

The "recipe" took on new devotees when John Hinerwadel Sr., a local postal carrier, purchased thirty-four acres and called it Hinerwadel's Grove. He farmed some of the land and, on the remainder, hosted clambakes, where Syracuse.com reports he brought in clams from the Chesapeake Bay. He took this simple potato preparation and served it as a side dish. They became an instant hit. So industrious was he that he began packaging the potatoes with a twelve-ounce bag of salt and labeled the package Hinerwadel's Famous Salt Potatoes. He contended that the perfect potato was a Size B Grade US No. 2 small new white potato. The salt ratio is important as well. Some recommend a cup of kosher coarse salt to six quarts of water; others feel you should first boil the water, add the salt and then the potatoes. The recipe here produced a Syracuse-worthy potato and tasted especially delicious when topped with a parsley-rich butter sauce.

•••••••••

Recipe: Salt Potatoes

This is a "no recipe" recipe but one you should add to your repertoire. Not only do the potatoes emerge with a salty crust and creamy center, but leftovers can be used in so many ways—think smashed potatoes, potato pancakes or hash browns.

Serves: 4
Start to finish: Under 30 minutes

½ cup kosher salt
1 ½ pounds new or Dutch potatoes (small are better than too large)
4 tablespoons (½ stick) butter
2 tablespoons of chopped flat-leaf parsley, optional
2 tablespoons chopped dill, optional

Fill a large pot with 8 cups (2 quarts) of cold water. Whisk in salt until the salt no longer settles on the bottom of the pot. Add potatoes, bring to a boil and then reduce to a simmer for 25–30 minutes, or until the potatoes can be easily pierced with a fork.

This is how you elevate a simple boiled potato, sour cream not needed, it's creamy enough. *Wikimedia Commons, Babil Sahoui.*

When the potatoes are nearly done, melt the butter in the microwave. When the potatoes are cooked through and tender, drain them thoroughly and let them sit for a few minutes for the salt to crystallize on the skins. Toss them in a bowl with the butter and chopped herbs if using.

Spiedies

The Abruzzo region is known for some of Italy's most delicious offerings. Their mortadella is legendary, their spaghetti "alla chitarra" is a classic and their saffron is so sublime that it comes with a special classification. So how is it that in Binghamton, New York, located in Broome County, immigrants from this region created a specialty that probably few residents in Abruzzo would even recognize? That's the tale of the spiedie sandwich, cubes of marinated meat served submarine style and brought to the fore of Binghamton cuisine by Italian immigrants from Abruzzo. These newcomers, according to Binghamton University, resided mainly in the Endicott neighborhood. In 1913, immigrants, more specifically Italian immigrants, were restricted in buying property. Those employed by Endicott-Johnson were aided in purchasing a home with land the company secured on the north side.

Through Endicott-Johnson, a vibrant Italian neighborhood thrived.

The name spiedie derives from the Italian *spiedo*, which means "kitchen cooking spit." Meat has been prepared in this age-old method since medieval times. When that same meat is marinated for hours or even days in what is essentially Italian dressing—a mixture of olive oil, vinegar and herbs such as oregano, dried basil, freshly cracked black pepper and garlic—the meat takes on a deep savory flavor. It is then enhanced by grilling, preferably over charcoal, for that rustic taste. The skewered meat, sometimes basted with additional marinade or a generous squeeze of fresh lemon, is coaxed off the skewer and enveloped in a waiting roll. The roots of this dish run deep in Binghamton, and the origin of the dish seems pretty certain. It is said that Camillo Iacovelli prepared the first spiedie and served them in his Endicott restaurant, the Parkview, back in 1938. The following year, his brother took the reins and sold them at his Endicott restaurant named Augie's. They called the original marinade "zuzu," and most likely it was lamb that was skewered and grilled. It was Augie's son, Guido, who continued the family legacy and was a prolific restaurateur. As with so many stories, there is one

It's all about the grill—use metal skewers or soak your bamboo ones to prevent them from igniting. *Unsplash, Joneshevchenko.*

other person who stakes a claim on originating the dish. That would be Peter Shark, who began serving them at his eponymous bar and grill in 1947. It does seem that the Iacovelli family predates this version.

The allure of a spiedie is easy to understand. It is familiar and familial, it evokes memories of childhood and simpler times and it is uncomplicated fare with a rich cultural connection and a taste of home.

Thousand Island Dressing

Shakespeare famously asked, What's in a name? Would a dressing called 1,854 small islands taste as sweet? If we're being geographically accurate, that's what we would call the mayonnaise-based dressing created in the Thousand Island region of New York. The area known as the Thousand Islands stretches from the northeast edge of Lake Ontario for nearly fifty miles along the St. Lawrence River to create a natural border between the United States and Canada. The 1,864 islands that comprise this archipelago make it one of the largest on the continent. The region has been a popular tourist destination since the mid-1800s, marked by its crystal waters and natural beauty.

Many, who are sorely misinformed, credit New York's Waldorf Astoria Hotel with creating the dressing that has become a popular choice for salads and a variety of food preparations. Certainly, the famed hotel helped popularize it, but they cannot take ownership. That status is almost unanimously credited to Sophia LaLonde of Clayton, New York. The story that most can agree on is that Sophia concocted the combination of mayonnaise and a variety of chopped add-ins to accompany the shore dinners that her husband, fisherman guide George, served at his fishing party shore dinners. According to *The Oxford Companion to American Food*, the recipe was shared with a New York stage actress named May Irwin who was also a cooking authority. Irwin then shared the recipe with others, and the dressing became a favorite. A second version, which still credits Sophia, says she shared it with summer resident George Boldt, who was the general manager of the Waldorf. He in turn presented it to his maître d'hôtel, the legendary Oscar Tschirky, and in 1894 it became a permanent menu item at the hotel's restaurant.

The culinary historians at the Food Timeline did a deep dive into Thousand Island dressing and how the recipe spread across the United States. They report that its first mention in print was in a 1912 Texas newspaper describing a lecturer named Miss Rich at the Texas State Fair who introduced fairgoers to the dressing. Recipes began appearing in newspapers across the country as its popularity spread. In 1912, the *Kansas City Star* published this version:

> Take one cup mayonnaise dressing, mix with one-half cut whipped cream, add small amount of Tarragon vinegar, one-half teaspoon of Imperial Sauce, then chop one hardboiled egg, one green pepper, one pimento, one pinch chives, mix well together and squeeze the juice of one lemon before serving. This sauce can be served with any kind of salad.

What once started as mayo, ketchup or chili sauce with bits of egg and onion can now include chopped olives, capers, parsley and green pepper. Noted food writer Craig Claiborne uncovered a recipe where chopped maraschino cherries, candied ginger or pineapple and pistachio nuts were added to the base.

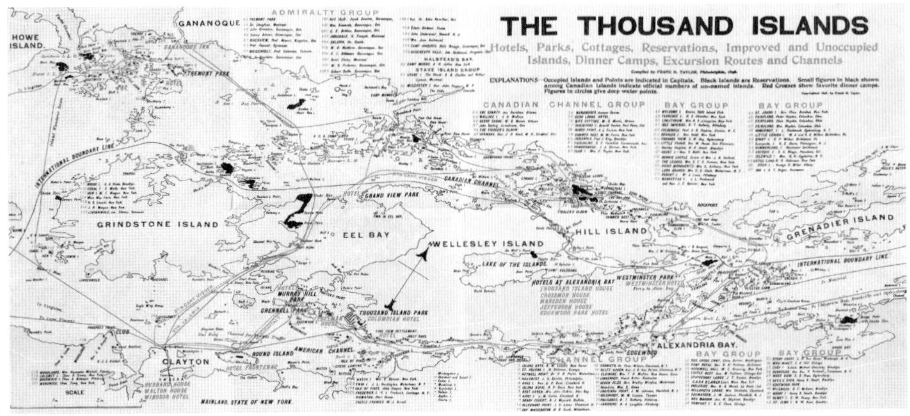

An international dressing named for a beautifully scenic area shared with our northern neighbor. *Wikimedia Commons, Frank H. Taylor.*

• • • • • • • • • •

Recipe: Deviled Eggs with Thousand Island Dressing

There are as many uses for the dressing as islands in the archipelago, but here's one of my favorite ways to incorporate it into a dish.

Makes: 12 halves
Start to finish: About 1 hour

6 large eggs
2 tablespoons mayonnaise
1 tablespoon ketchup
2 teaspoons sweet green relish
Kosher salt and freshly cracked black pepper to taste
Optional garnishes: olives, capers, pickles, paprika

Place the eggs in a medium pot and fill with water to cover. Bring to a boil over medium to high heat; this should take about 15 minutes. When the water boils, cover the pot and remove it from the stove. Let the eggs sit in the steamy water for 13 minutes for a hard-cooked egg. After that time, place the eggs in a cold-water bath for 30–60 minutes (this prevents a ring from forming around the yolk and makes peeling easier). Peel the eggs under cold running water.

While the eggs cook, in a small bowl prepare the Thousand Island dressing. Mix the mayonnaise, ketchup and relish together. Season to taste with salt and pepper.

Let the eggs dry on a paper towel and then slice in half lengthwise. Pop out the yolks into the bowl with the dressing. Mash thoroughly to create a smooth spread. Spoon or pipe the mixture into the egg halves. You can then serve as is or top with optional garnish.

UTICA GREENS

You might think that Utica greens is a new crayon color, but you'd be incorrect. Like so many culinary contributions of Upstate New York, this spicy dish that combines leafy greens with a variety of mix-ins was born of the ingenuity of frugal immigrant cooks. Central New York was home to a large Italian immigrant community who brought with them a farm-to-table attitude long before the phrase was coined. They came mainly from southern Italy to work in the Upstate mills and on railroad construction. To stretch the budget, they used what they had and infused it with culinary techniques from their homeland. Escarole, or as an Italian *nonna* might say, "scarole," was a staple in the backyard gardens of East Utica. For those who have never had the pleasure of eating escarole, its taste is a cross between bitter chicory and a more subtle green like romaine. Utica greens were typical comfort food—that is, until Joe Morelle brought them to a wider market.

Joe Morelle (who was name-dropped in the chicken riggies section) was a chef in the 1970s heyday of Italian American Upstate chefs. Many, like Joe, worked at a local haunt called Grimaldi's, which opened in Utica back in 1943. Morelle took his cooking chops next to Chesterfields, where he created and popularized this at-home favorite. Joe's version, which was a featured recipe in the *New York Times* cooking section, uses prosciutto not sausage, hot cherry peppers and a gremolata-like topping made from grated Parmigiano cheese, breadcrumbs and olive oil. Jim Shahin of the *Times* noted that in Utica they're not called Utica greens. He quoted the owner of Chesterfields, Sal Borruso, who quipped, "Somebody calls here and says they want Utica greens, I tell them we don't have those." Simply known as "greens Morelle," this dish's fame never really left the region. Borruso went on to say that Utica was known as much for its corruption as for these greens, noting that

16 F. W. BOLGIANO & CO.,

EGG PLANT

Large, Oval, Dark, Glossy, Purple Egg Plant.

(EIERFRUCHT.)

✓**Large, Oval, Dark, Glossy, Purple, Thornless Egg Plant.**—In shape, color and size this egg plant is perfection. Its rich, glossy, dark purple color, its beautiful form and large size makes it most attractive for the markets and for shipping. Experienced gardeners discard all other sorts, giving this decided preference. It is earlier than other sorts, and outsells all other varieties. Packets, 5c. and 10c. ½ ounce, 15c. Ounce, 25c. ¼ pound, 90c. Pound, $3.50.

✓**Large New York Improved Spineless Egg Plant.**—Packets, 5c. and 10c. Ounce, 25c. ¼ pound 90c. Pound $3.50.

ONE OUNCE EGG PLANT SEED WILL PRODUCE 500 PLANTS.

Egg plant seed should be sown very early in hot-beds the plants being very tender must be protected from frost, but exposed so far as practicable to light and air to harden them. Egg plant seed will not germinate freely without a strong uniform heat, if they get the least chilled they seldom recover, therefor repeated sowings are sometimes necessary.

ENDIVE. (Endivien.)

One ounce will sow 150 feet of row.

Endive is one of the best salads for fall and winter use. Sow for an early supply about the middle of April. As it is used mostly in the fall months, the main sowings are made in June and July. Plant one foot apart each way. When the plant has attained its full size gather up the leaves and tie them by their tips in a conical form. This excludes the light and air from the inner leaves until blanched.

✓**Green Curled.**—*Self-Bleaching.*—The best in cultivation. Much more beautiful and ornamental than the old sort. Packets, 5c. and 10c. Ounce, 20c. ¼ pound, 50c. Pound, $1.50.

Escarole or Broadleaved Endive.—Leaves a pale green—requires very little blanching. More productive than green curled. Forms large heads of broad, thick leaves. Packets, 5c. and 10c. Ounce, 20c. ¼ pound, 50c. Pound, $1.50.

Green Curled Self-Blanching Endive.

HERBS.—(Krauter.)

New American Majoram Sweet.—A perennial plant, but not hardy enough to endure the winter of the North. The young tender tops are used green for flavoring, or they may be dried for winter use. Sow in drills as early as possible, and thin out the plants to ten inches. Packets, 5c. and 10c. Ounce, 20c.

Sweet Basil.—A hardy annual from the East Indies. The seed and stem are used for flavoring soups and sauces, having the flavor of cloves. Packets, 5c. and 10c. Ounce, 20c. Pound, $1.25.

Sage.—A hardy perennial possessing some medicinal properties, but cultivated principally for use as a condiment, it being used more extensively than any other herb for flavoring and dressing. Sow early in the spring (4 to 5 pounds to the acre in drills) on very rich ground, cultivate often and thin the plants to 16 inches apart. Cut the leaves and tender shoots just as the plant is coming into flower and dry quickly in the shade. The plants will survive the winter and may be divided. If this is done they will give a second crop superior in quality. Packets, 5c. and 10c. Ounce, 20c. Pound, $2.00.

Mammoth Dill.—Our Mammoth Dill grows much larger than the old sorts, and is in every way superior and preferable. Packets, 5c. and 10c. ¼ pound, 20c. Pound, 75.

Lavender.—The leaves of this plant are used for seasoning and the flowers for perfumery. When seed is sown it should be planted when the apple is in bloom. Packets, 5c. and 10c. Ounce 20c. ¼ pound, 50c. Pound $1.50.

Broad Leaf English Thyme.—This herb is perennial, and is both a medicinal and culinary plant The young leaves and tops are used for soups, dressing and sauce. A tea is made of the leaves which is a great remedy in nervous headache. Sow as early as the ground will permit. Packets, 5c. and 10c. Ounce, 25c. Pound, $3.00.

Summer Savory.—A hardy annual, the dried stems, leaves and flowers of which are extensively used for flavoring, particularly in dressings and soups. Culture the same as that of sweet majoriam. Packets, 5c. and 10c. Ounce, 15c. Pound, $1.00.

Culture.—Select light, rich soil and lay off in shallow drills one foot apart, along which sprinkle the seed and cover slightly. Do not let the plants stand closer than two or three inches.

A 1902 catalogue page to help any nonna worth her salt plant a garden where herbs, veggies and escarole could grow. *Wikimedia Commons, F.W. Bolgiano & Co. Henry G. Gilbert Nursery and Seed Trade Catalog Collection.*

in the restaurant, "You knew everybody. On this half was the FBI. That half, wise guys." Utica greens has now become a favorite chef-driven dish where it is named for the chef who tweaks the recipe. From "greens Ralph" to "greens Sal," the ingredients might differ, salami instead of prosciutto, potatoes making an appearance or a topping with panko instead of crumbs. At its heart, it is an homage to the home cooks of the late 1800s who were resourceful and creative and made a dish that has stood the test of time.

For recommendations on where you can find these notable dishes, visit the "Where to Go" section at the back of the book.

Honorable Mention

There are the iconic thirteen that you just read about and then there are some dishes that haven't quite reached iconic status but are definitely an Upstate thing. Those are listed here and deserve honorable mention.

Tapping Into Upstate History

I hope you remember that wayward tomahawk that landed in a maple tree and sweetened up food for New York's Native Americans, as it was only one chapter ago. That serendipitous event created a thriving industry in Upstate New York that still exists today. New York produces upward of 820,000 gallons of maple syrup annually, making it the second-largest producer of the sweet sticky stuff in the country, second only to Vermont. Currently, according to the New York State Maple Association, there are over 2,000 sugar makers in the state who tap into the sustainable crop every year.

No matter how you bottle it, if it's New York maple syrup, it'll be sweet and delicious. *Unsplash, Nadine Primea.*

Duck, Duck, Goose

Currently, there are three purveyors of luxury foie gras in the United States, and two of them are in the Catskill region of New York. Together, Hudson Valley foie gras and La Belle annually sell upward of $40 million of the decadently unctuous product. They both market foie (connoisseurs call it by its first name only) from the Moulard (mulard) duck. This variety is a cross between a typical white farm duck, the Pekin, and a South American breed known as Muscovy. The Moulard innately stores fat in the liver, making them uniquely positioned to provide foie gras (French for "fatty liver"). On their farms in the Catskills, they each ethically raise ducks to produce this high-end luxury food product. Efforts in New York City under Mayor Bill DeBlasio tried to ban the sale of foie, citing it as an inhumane product. Making the sale illegal would not only shut down these farms but also have a dramatic ripple effect throughout the Upstate region, which relies on this industry. That's why the Catskill Foie Gras Collective fought the ban and seemed to have won a victory as 2022 ended. The New York State Department of Agriculture and Markets has ruled with them, stating the ban is a violation of state law. There is sure to be more back and forth on the issue, but for now, production is still in full swing. If the taste profile of the country is indicative, it shows no sign of slowing down.

Cornell Ruled the Roost

Cornell is known not only as a center for higher learning but also as an innovator of some popular breakthrough foods. Leading the roost was professor of poultry science Robert C. Baker, whose role at Cornell was to innovate new ways to use New York poultry. His most famous or dubious contribution was perfecting the chicken nugget. It was Baker who in 1963 found a way to get breadcrumbs to adhere to the small bites and remain intact through the deep-frying process. He found that if you ground the raw chicken, drew out its moisture and added a binder they could hold their nugget form. He froze, dipped and dredged using eggs and breadcrumbs, with a second freezing after the process. He and his colleagues packaged them as chicken sticks and sold them to local markets. His discovery was widely published, and Baker gave away his trade secrets. Baker noted in an interview with the *Ithaca Journal* that at first, they weren't too popular. Now, chicken nuggets can be found in every frozen food section and famously in McDonald's Happy Meals.

Baker's recipe for a barbecue sauce might be his most popular food achievement. As early as 1949, Baker had a food concession at the Syracuse-based New York State Fair, where Baker's Chicken Coop featured his barbecue formula. The sauce, which he used as a marinade and basting sauce, was a simple combination of oil, cider vinegar, egg and seasoning. Cornell's College of Agriculture and Life Sciences reports that his seasonal stand served "nearly 1,000 half-chickens (a.k.a. 'broilers') a day for two weeks in late summer. It's said that former President Bill Clinton was a fan noting he bypassed New York State apples for the savory bird, commenting, 'Those apples look good, but where's the chicken?'" Baker became a member of the American Poultry Hall of Fame, as he not only innovated these two chicken recipes but also engineered vacuum packaging for poultry, created

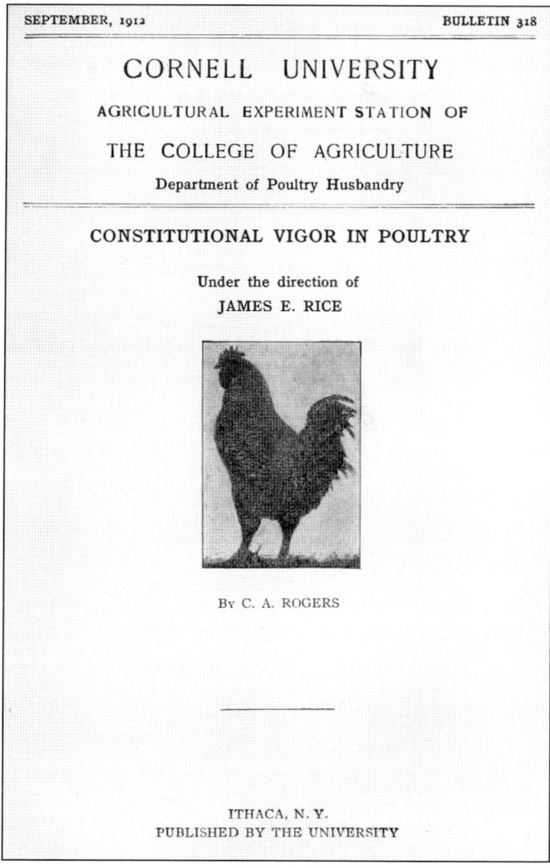
SEPTEMBER, 1912 BULLETIN 318

CORNELL UNIVERSITY

AGRICULTURAL EXPERIMENT STATION OF

THE COLLEGE OF AGRICULTURE

Department of Poultry Husbandry

CONSTITUTIONAL VIGOR IN POULTRY

Under the direction of
JAMES E. RICE

By C. A. ROGERS

ITHACA, N. Y.
PUBLISHED BY THE UNIVERSITY

Cornell was the center for advancements in agriculture and poultry development. *Cornell University.*

"turkey ham" and developed poultry hotdogs. Baker's goal from the start of his career was to increase profitability for New York's chicken farmers. While he never made millions from his creations, he accomplished what he wanted and secured Upstate New York's place in the history of chicken, no paltry feat!

• • • • • • • • • •

Recipe: Cornell Chicken

The least guarded secret recipe on the internet is the one for Cornell chicken, with almost every recipe exactly replicating what Dr. Baker created. That's because if it ain't broke, don't fix it. The chicken is best when grilled over hot charcoal, and Dr. Baker used whole chickens that were halved. You can use your favorite method for grilling or roasting and your favorite parts. Here's the basis for the famous basting sauce. Note that Baker did not intend it to be a marinade, although many recipes suggest just that.

1 egg
1 cup cooking oil
2 cups cider vinegar
3 tablespoons salt
1 tablespoon poultry seasoning (if yours contains salt, reduce the amount above)
½ teaspoon black pepper
2 whole broilers, halved

Beat the egg, then whisk in the oil. When combined, stir in the remaining ingredients. Grill the chicken halves over hot charcoal after the flame has died out. Turn the chicken parts over every 10 minutes, brushing the basting sauce on each time. Grill for about 1 hour, or until an instant-read thermometer inserted in the thigh reads 165 degrees. Discard any unused sauce.

Taking a Dip

I can tell you that mozzarella sticks, the darlings of Italian eateries, and melba sauce, that refined puree of raspberries created by premier

French chef Auguste Escoffier, are routinely eaten together in Albany, New York. I'm not saying that a patron enjoys a plate of mozzarella sticks and then orders vanilla ice cream with melba sauce for dessert. No, they are eaten in tandem, with the former being dipped into the latter. You might wonder, how many beers do you need to drink to find this combination not just palatable but crave-worthy? Those who scoff are pointed to baked brie smothered in a peach glaze or the delight of a piece of camembert with fig jam. So, they maintain it's not hard to understand the attraction of dipping a freshly fried gooey piece of breaded cheese into the cloyingly sweet sauce. How it started as a practice might remain a mystery. However, Leanne Ricchiuti plunged into the origin of this combo for civmix.com. Her dogged investigative reporting would make Deep Throat of Watergate notoriety cringe with embarrassment for his lack of effort. Leanne, after much hunting, tracking and googling, found that the dish originated outside of New York but was popularized at H.P. Mulligan's, where it prominently appeared on the menu as battered mozzarella with a great raspberry sauce ($2.95). She even has a newspaper article dating back to 1982 with a review of Mulligan's to confirm the report. As Leanne writes, BOOM.

Chicken French

Despite its French-sounding name, Chicken French, the battered and lightly sauteed chicken breasts in a sauce of lemon, butter and wine, is decidedly an Italian American creation. It's a riff on Veal Francese, which gained popularity in NYC and was served in both neighborhood and swanky Italian restaurants. Its association with Rochester came from its preparation at the Brown Derby, a favorite haunt for many in Rochester seeking straightforward and well-prepared Italian dishes. James Cianciola, a.k.a. Chef Vincenzo, is widely credited as being the first to put the dish on a menu. Getting pushback from customers about the use of veal, Chef Vincenzo substituted chicken at the restaurant, which was located on Monroe Avenue in Brighton. The preparation was so popular that they decided to "French" some other menu items, such as artichokes, cauliflower and haddock. They ran with the concept and even wrote a book called *Frenching Food Italian Style*, with seventy-three recipes from the restaurant. In the introduction to the book, Nate, Vincenzo's brother, tells warm stories about his deep Italian roots while growing up in a section of Rochester called "the lots," so named for the gardens most Italian immigrants had in their backyards. Ironically, it was their veal, not Chicken Francese that earned Nate an international award. You know you've reached the pinnacle of success when the *New York Times* cooking section publishes a variation on your recipe and it makes the list of the most popular recipes of the year. That happened in 2018 when Julia Moskin presented Chicken Francese, noting that some call it Chicken French. Those some would be Rochester natives who were lucky enough to have sampled the original.

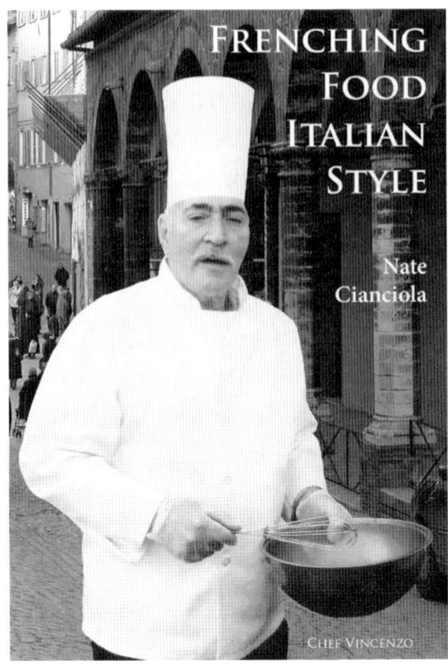

Chef Vincenzo and his brother Nate collaborated to bring Francese food to the masses. *Author photo.*

Subbing In

Some dishes seem to invent themselves. That might just be the case with chicken finger subs, a sandwich made popular in Buffalo and one now imitated by anyone who knows what good food is. In his love letter to Western New York food, *Buffalo Everything: A Guide to Eating in "The Nickel City"*, Arthur Bovino described the sandwich, "where chicken fingers slip off children's menus and into soft Costanzo's sub rolls with provolone, tomato, lettuce, blue cheese dressing, and Frank's Red Hot sauce to become something truly naughty: crunchy, spicy, and messy—too naughty for kids." The sub was purportedly the creation of John's Pizza & Subs in Tonawanda, sometime in the 1980s. The sandwich is a mashup of a chicken parm wedge and Buffalo wings meet chicken fingers. The roll Bovino references comes from none other than Costanzo's, a bakery located along the Niagara River. They've been baking bread for the Buffalo area since 1933. Like all good food stories, other restaurants say they were the first to invent the sandwich. Today, you can find it on almost every Buffalo menu worth its red sauce.

Mozzarella Mountain

Sprinkling Parmesan cheese on top of your spaghetti certainly is not unique. However, draping your bowl of spaghetti in a mound of melted mozzarella cheese is another thing. That's the no. 1 seller at Chef's, a Buffalo standard bearer for Italian food. According to Louis Bilittier Jr., the proprietor and chef at this decades-old family restaurant, the dish was created when his father had lunch with TV host Dave Thomas. Wanting to experiment with their usual bowl of spaghetti in red sauce, they added a copious amount of butter to the sauce and a mountain of mozzarella cheese on top. The dish was then placed under the broiler for an ooey, gooey slightly browned finish. Spaghetti parm is still going strong more than six decades later, Bilittier says, serving over one thousand plates a month.

I'm Stuffed

Let's linger in Buffalo's Italian food contributions just long enough to enjoy stuffed banana peppers. No doubt, stuffing a pepper is not unique to Western New York or, for that matter, to Italian cooks. However, how Buffalonians stuff and enjoy theirs is unique to the area. *Buffalo Spree* magazine, which is focused on Western New York, looked deeply into the banana pepper phenomenon and has proclaimed it to be a Buffalo specialty. Thought to have been invented and perfected by Chef Andrew Divincenzo at Bill Ogden's in Lovejoy, the pepper has the usual suspects of breadcrumbs, cheese and seasoning all stuffed into a banana or other pepper. Divincenzo achieved a fair amount of attention as he and his recipe were featured in print and on air. He was a regular at the annual Taste of the NFL, and when he passed, he was memorialized in the U.S. House of Representatives. There is a caution that comes with eating the stuffed specialty: as Bovino warned, "They can be 'Russian roulette-spicy.'" You never know if the one you are biting into is tame or hot, so eaters beware.

Wash It All Down

When you are done trying all these singular Upstate foods and find yourself in need of a thirst quencher, you might reach for a Buffalo favorite, a Loganberry. This somewhat syrupy sweet noncarbonated drink was first enjoyed at Crystal Beach Park just over the Canadian border in the late 1800s, when Buffalonians boarded a ferry and headed for the shores of Lake Erie. Its taste is a cross between the blackberry and raspberry, and it was named for James Harvey Logan. You would be hard-pressed to find Loganberry sold anywhere outside of Western New York, so next time you're there, score a can or enjoy a milkshake flavored with loganberry syrup.

Chapter 3

FESTIVALS, FAIRS AND FOOD

After discovering some of Upstate's iconic foods, it seems natural to explore the fairs and festivals that celebrate them. If the concept of a festival or fair conjures up an image of jousting knights, juggling jesters and a prayer or two, then you are either a medieval history buff, watching too much television or perhaps both. At their inception, fairs and festivals were gatherings with pomp, circumstance and a religious focus. That makes sense, as the word *fair* derives from the Latin word *feria*, meaning "festival" or "holy day." These gatherings, often organized by the church, attracted merchants across Europe to show and sell their wares. It was also an opportunity for villagers to enjoy a respite from work, as entertainment and food soon became popular additions to these open-air events. Fairs have evolved over the years, but their primary goals haven't changed. They strive to celebrate and elevate local food and hope to create a food focused religious experience. The distinction of the oldest continuous running fair in the United States goes to the Steuben County Fair in Bath, New York. Fair manager Nick Pelham is proud of this Southern Tier institution that dates back to 1795. Steuben set the stage for the plethora of fairs that distinguish Upstate New York. There are too many to list and delve into, but a few that stand out for their uniqueness are highlighted here. They tell us so much about local pride and encapsulate the spirit of the Upstate personality.

Mangia

Highmark Stadium, the home of the Buffalo Bills, routinely sees contests that require grit and determination. They involve a motivated offense and a strong defense. In this encounter that takes place every Labor Day weekend, the offense is an overuse of Frank's hot sauce and the only line of defense is a wet nap. That's because the contest on the field involves Buffalo wings, and the goal is to eat the most. The festival began as a figment of Bill Murray's imagination. His character Frank Detorre in the cult film *Osmosis Jones* is addicted to fried foods and heads to Buffalo for a chicken wing festival. At the time, in 2002, no such festival existed. In reaction to this lightbulb moment, Chef Drew Cerza, dubbed the "Wing King," founded the festival, which to date has served over 5.5 million wings to more than 1 million attendees. The extra point is the charitable aspect, which has raised considerable funds for local charities. If you think you have what it takes to enter the amateur, college or hot-wing contests, head to Buffalo in the fall. Be sure to bring plenty of napkins and a bib if you plan on joining the bobbing for wing arena.

Hang on to those napkins, you'll need them when you combine a hot air balloon rally with a popular Binghamton food. Spiedie Fest, a celebration of the popular and local Italian sandwich, draws over 100,000 visitors annually in August. This festival takes these two disparate attractions and brings them together for a three-day event. And because the sponsors of

A wing-loving crowd at Coca-Cola Field in Buffalo anxiously waiting for the "Wing King" to be crowned. *Wikimedia Commons, Fortunate4now.*

the event felt it needed another curious addition, the thirty-eighth festival spotlighted professional wrestling, with former WWE and current AEW stars participating. Let's not forget the star of the show is the spiedie. These delectable sandwiches round out the event in a spicy way.

While we are highlighting Italian foods of the region, head to Utica for Riggiefest, Tomato Pie Day and Utica Greens Fest. These classic Italian specialties are celebrated with local competitions, copious amounts of food and live music. Riggiefest, which was started in 2005 as a fundraiser for the YWCA of the Mohawk Valley, sponsors the festival to determine the best chicken riggies in the area. Teddy's, which has won the competition countless times, gracefully bowed out of the competition after being inducted into the Riggie Hall of Fame. Tomato pie also has its moment to shine, and attendees can sample tomato pie entries. I can attest to the quality of the winningest establishment, Roma Sausage & Deli, where tomato pie is elevated to an art form. And should you need just one more reason to visit Utica, you can attend the Greens Fest, which brings local music and arts together and throws Utica greens in for good measure. It's a way to get both your cultural and culinary fixes all in one place.

Sauerkraut

If you're looking for a more pungent experience, head to Phelps, a town in Ontario County. You won't need GPS; just follow your nose as it leads you to the epicenter of sauerkraut production. This 180-plus-year-old town, which sits between Rochester and Syracuse, at one time produced nearly one-third of all the sauerkraut in the United States. According to a 1973 article in the *New York Times*, that came to about 100 million pounds of the fermented cabbage. Sauerkraut has quite the history; reportedly, it was fuel for the laborers who built the Great Wall of China, and let's remember that was before port-a-potties were invented. Phelps developed as a hub when two major sauerkraut processors were located there. While those businesses have since left, sauerkraut has such a legacy in Phelps that it is still celebrated. That's a good thing for its six thousand residents. If you plan on visiting for the annual festival held in August, you can take part in a "Kraut Krawl," cabbage head decorating or bowling and a sauerkraut recipe contest. It makes for a tangy weekend away.

You can follow your nose or this sign announcing the sauerkraut festival. *visitfingerlakes.com.*

Onions, Garlic and Burgers

It's not a far cry from Phelps to Elba, a town in Genesee County, but the trip there just might make you teary-eyed. Elba is the self-proclaimed onion capital of the country. The mucky soil is very hospitable to growing onions, but the truth is, several other states are more prolific in the endeavor. That hasn't stopped Elba from hosting, since 1937, its annual August festival. Oniony foods are not in short supply, from onion rings and sausage and onions to onion soup and the "blooming onion" made popular by a national restaurant chain. Of course, there's an onion queen and lots of local pride. An unverified report says that while campaigning for president, Harry S. Truman passed through Elba and made a comment, based on the aroma, that it should more aptly be called Smelba!

If onions make you hungry for more from the allium family, drive straight from Elba to Geneva, Seneca County. There, you can sample New York garlic in all its forms. Over the last few decades, Upstate New York has become known for its garlic production growing at higher rates than carrots, cabbage, lettuce or onions. This commodity, which can go from pungent to buttery sweet when it converts from its raw state to cooked, is celebrated not only in Geneva but also annually in Saugerties, Ulster County. There, the "stinking rose," as it is lovingly termed, is elevated through dozens of farmers and vendors who glorify and sanctify this versatile bulb. From cooking demos to how to grow garlic in your backyard, you might never look at garlic the same way again.

If your happy meal is a burger, then your next destination should be the Hamburger Festival in Hamburg, New York, where the food court features everything you'd expect in a burger fest. It's no coincidence that this Erie County city celebrates the burger; as you read, they have a credible claim to its creation back in 1885. This charitable event, which supports local organizations, is filled with music and entertainment for one day smack dab in the center of Hamburg on Main and Buffalo Streets. If you need to round out your meal, there's pizza, ice cream and a beer tent where a cold brew will awaken you from your meat coma.

The Sweet Stuff

A little more kind on your arteries is the Busti apple festival held in the fall in Chautauqua County. This festival, which is nearly half a century old, celebrates the robust apple industry and features a working gristmill, vendors and an endless supply of apple pie and cider. Busti is a ripe example of the local nature of a festival. A little-known and totally off-topic fact about Busti is its connection to the abolitionist movement and the Underground Railroad. Busti counted over thirty formerly enslaved residents who used their homes and farms to aid in the movement of those escaping slavery. It's a fascinating aspect of this quiet rural county.

As long as we're on your sweet side, let's visit the Eden Corn Festival, also held in August when the kernels are their sweetest. This festival has been held annually since 1963, when corn sold for ten cents an ear and a whopping six thousand ears were sold. There's a corn queen, corn judging and, I am sure, a plethora of corny puns. If you want a popping good time (there's one now), this would be the festival for you.

This brings us to the grape festival set in Naples, New York, which first began in 1857. Known for its grape production, the region celebrates the grape with a pie contest and offerings from puddings to pastries, jams and jellies. To honor the legacy of Irene Bouchard, a local market sponsors a grape pie contest at the festival, where winners receive a cash prize and the Irene Bouchard Trophy. As Naples is located in the heart of the Finger Lakes Wine region, you can also be sure that the grape in all its drinkable forms will be in abundance. Known for the purple liquid, Naples was a celebrated stop for New York Senator Robert Kennedy. He was photographed picking grapes right off the vine as he favorably compared the wines he sampled to those of France and Italy. If you do

This grape picker circa 1925 plays a crucial role in the process. *Wikimedia Commons.*

This 1898 image illustrates a man tapping a hard maple on the property of Seth Chapin in Chenango County. *Wikimedia Commons.*

attend, be sure to sport your best purple clothing, as that is the color of the day.

Another sweet surprise includes the maple syrup festivals held in March, when tapping season begins. The annual attractions are hosted by New York State maple producers, who invite you to tour their "sugar houses" and sample their liquid gold. If you are wondering just how many pancakes or waffles can be eaten in a weekend, then you don't understand the breadth of what maple syrup can do. There's maple butter, taffy, maple cream and a boozy maple liqueur. Unlike many other artisanal foods that require tremendous training and expertise, the NYS Maple Association helps the amateur get started without unnecessarily tapping their resources. One needs a good drill and a spile, which is a peg or spigot. You'll need to have a bucket, storage containers and equipment to boil the sap. A thermometer and filter are helpful tools. While you're at it, you can certainly succumb to the cliché and enjoy a pancake breakfast. Just be sure you never admit to having ever used that corn syrupy confection that masquerades as maple syrup—it might get you booted out of the area.

Nearly every county across the country hosts these regional and local events. They are an amazing way to not only sample local cuisine but also get a true taste of local pride. Next time you're looking for a way to immerse yourself in the culture of a region, consider attending a fair or festival. I'd argue that much like the first fairs held before the calendar recorded time, it can be a religious experience. For more suggestions, visit the "Where to Go" section at the back of the book.

Chapter 4

THE CANAL'S CULINARY CULTURE

I've got a mule and her name is Sal
Fifteen years on the Erie Canal
She's a good old worker and a good old pal
Fifteen years on the Erie Canal
We've hauled some barges in our day
Filled with lumber coal and hay
And every inch of the way we know
From Albany to Buffalo
—Folk song, 1905

The canal, a waterway initially only forty feet wide by four feet deep, was the first to connect the Atlantic Seaboard with the vast territory to the west. The canal opened up commerce while positioning New York City's port as the most prosperous in the country. Freight costs were reduced by 95 percent, and states to the west of New York—including Michigan, Wisconsin, Minnesota, Illinois and Indiana—saw a boom in population and industry as a direct result of the canal. Few innovations have led to more prosperity and more significatly affected the broad access to food than the construction of the Erie Canal. There were many people instrumental in the development of the Erie Canal, one being Elkanah Watson. Watson was not a native New Yorker, but in 1789, he made Albany his home. He was an agriculturist and businessman and a progressive thinker who identified the need for a waterway. In his book *The Travels of Elkanah Watson*,

Jeremy Dupertuis Bangs chronicled Watson's endeavors from meeting the Marquis de Lafayette to his tours of England, where their canal system imprinted on him. He served as a courier for George Washington and an emissary of Benjamin Franklin, so his résumé was quite impressive. He was engaged in the concept of canal travel and maintained that it was he, not senator of New York DeWitt Clinton, who spearheaded the idea of building the canal.

A stately portrait of Elkanah Watson. *NYPL Digital Collections.*

Watson might have been the motivator, but it wasn't until several years later that another social influencer, Jesse Hawley, played a more tangible role in canal development. To provide context, in the late eighteenth and early nineteenth centuries, New York was awash with wheat. One town, Esopus in Ulster County, has been singled out for its wheat fields, which were described in the writings of U.P. Hedrick, a noted botanist and horticulturist who wrote extensively on the topic. He referred to the area as a "very beautiful and fertile wheatland which here grows so abundantly that this Esopus is the granary of the whole New Netherlands." Shortly after the American Revolution, Upstate New York emerged as the center of wheat production in the country. Regions such as Hudson, Mohawk, Susquehanna and Genesee Valleys were especially prolific in wheat's production and milling it into flour. Hawley was one such miller who had a supply chain issue with how to get his milled wheat to market. With a lack of transportation, Hawley's flour languished and he fell into debt, landing him in debtor's prison in Ontario County. There, under the pseudonym "Hercules," Hawley published a series of fourteen essays arguing for the construction of a canal from Buffalo to Albany. Those essays did not go unnoticed and have been considered an additional spark for the canal's construction.

Senator DeWitt Clinton is widely credited for taking the canal's potential and running with it. The endeavor, which was labeled "Clinton's folly" or derided as "Clinton's ditch," was turned aside by President Thomas

Top: A rendering of DeWitt Clinton mingling the waters of Lake Erie and the Atlantic. *NYPL Digital Collections.*

Bottom: Photo of the Erie Canal at Little Falls. *Library of Congress, Detroit Publishing.*

Jefferson, so it fell on Upstate New York to carve out the 363 miles of canal. The canal building began on July 4, 1817, in Rome, New York. Construction was rapid and arduous, being dug almost completely by hand and relying heavily on local and Irish immigrant labor. It took a mere eight years at a cost of $7 million to complete. In a symbolic ceremony, then Governor Clinton boarded a vessel called the *Seneca Chief* and traveled down the canal to New York City. There, he was said to have poured fresh water that he carried with him from Lake Erie into the Atlantic Ocean, ostensibly forever tying the two together. The ceremony dubbed "Wedding of the Waters" signaled the great potential the canal presented.

A FOOD JOURNEY

I would wager to say that there is no current authority more knowledgeable of the Erie Canal's effect on foodways than Derrick Pratt. Derrick, in his capacity as director of education for the Erie Canal Museum, created a project devoted solely to this endeavor. The canal has generally been viewed through the lens of a marvel of engineering, but it was so much more in its effect on Upstate New York's relationship with the food it produced, created and marketed. It defined an immigrant experience, an entrepreneurial streak and a breakthrough moment for Upstate New York. As Pratt described in *Erie Eats*, "Agriculture, industry, social life, government, and culture were all tremendously impacted by the convergence of the Erie Canal with foodways, as they also influenced how the Canal and communities along its banks developed."

Before the canal, shipping products from Upstate New York was a challenge. Prior to construction, for anything to get from point A to point B, you had to traverse the Appalachian Mountains, which run through the region. This obstacle to transport created logjams of shipments, high costs and inefficacy. Before the canal, New York's abundance of wheat was stalled. It could take nearly a month for a shipment from Buffalo to reach New York City and cost a staggering one hundred dollars, which at the time was prohibitive. With the canal in place, New York could now ship wheat at one-tenth the cost, which certainly would have kept Hawley out of debtor's prison. In the crop's heyday, mills sprouted up along the banks of the canal, creating prosperity and employment. Companies such as Gold Medal Flour and General Mills based themselves in the Rochester area. While New York City might have introduced America to bagels, it is likely the milled flour came from Upstate New York. As Western states took advantage of this new route to market, New York's wheat was no longer competitive, and the need to develop other markets arose. Pratt explained, "The canal with its efficiency, competition, easy communication, and spirit of optimism, transformed the Canal Corridor into a natural incubator for innovation, especially in its largest industry: agriculture."

Farms, often manned by enslaved labor, began to rely on fruits, vegetables and dairy to make up for the lost wheat business. Specialty farms sprang up, with those in Phelps and Rochester showcasing cabbage and sauerkraut, Lyons growing peppermint and Canastota celery and onions. Rochester went from being the "flour city" to the "flower city" as nurseries dotted the landscape. The canal aided the salt industry in Central New York. After the canal was opened, New York was said to produce nearly 90 percent of the nation's salt.

ADVERTISEMENTS.

THE ONONDAGA

Coarse Salt Association,

MANUFACTURERS AND DEALERS IN ALL KINDS OF

GOARSE OR SOLAR SALT,

F. F. Dairy, Table, Common, Fine and Fertilizing Salts.

General Office No. 1 Clinton Block, SYRACUSE, N. Y.

THOMAS K. GALE, *President.* THOMAS MOLLOY, *Treasurer and Secretary.*
W. H. H. GERE, *Vice-President.* LEWIS A. HAWLEY, *Rec. Secretary.*

TRUSTEES:

G. C. GERE, SAMUEL THOMPSON, HORACE K. WHITE,
W. B. BOYD, W. KIRKPATRICK, GEO. F. COMSTOCR, Jr.,
W. H. H. GERE, THEODORE L. POOLE, D. W. PECK,
LEWIS A HAWLEY, PATRICK LYNCH, THOS. K. GALE,
THOS G. ALVORD, E. L. LUDDINGTON. THOS. P. MURRAY,
PHILIP CORKINGS, THOMAS MOLLOY, A. C. BELDEN,
JAMES M. GERE, DANIEL PRATT, NEWELL E. LOOMIS.
MYRON C. MERRIMAN, Jr.

THOMAS MOLLOY,

—RECEIVER OF—

The American Dairy Salt Co., Lt'd,

General Office No. 1 Clinton Block,

SYRACUSE, N. Y.

An advertisement dated 1893 that appeared in *Boyd's Syracuse City Directory*. *Wikimedia Commons.*

Necessity was truly the mother of invention when the foods that were being grown needed to be preserved. New technology developed, and canneries and food processing plants sporting these advancements were hallmarks of the region. A cannery in Syracuse that began processing vegetables in 1868 blossomed into a company with twenty-six canning factories and produced a product known as None Such. This condensed mincemeat could give Spam a run for its money. Beech-Nut, the company known for its baby food and chewing gum, started as a cannery in Canajoharie in 1891. They patented their sealed jars used to store, of all things, bacon. Speaking of bacon, meatpacking plants, often introduced by German immigrants, such as the Hofmann Sausage Company, were also a canal success story.

The influence the canal had on alcohol production is not to be overlooked. The Genesee and Mohawk Valleys were perfectly positioned to grow barley and corn for whiskey. The Finger Lakes had the right conditions for wine, the Lake Ontario region excelled in cider and Central New York was optimal for hops. Shipping these fresh products could be troublesome, but turn them into consumable alcohol and you've outsmarted Mother Nature. Farmers pivoted, and the canal evolved. Pratt noted that many canal workers were paid in alcohol, albeit the amount they could consume was often rationed to twelve to twenty ounces per day. Without the aid of Indeed.com, the job of "jigger boss" was filled, as he was empowered to loosen the rations if productivity increased. Drinking was also prevalent in towns along the canal, especially those located by the locks. It is quite possible that the excessive drinking on the canal provoked the temperance movement, as two supporters of the Eighteenth Amendment, Elizabeth Cady Stanton and Susan B. Anthony, were what Pratt calls "women within the Canal Corridor." Ironically, during Prohibition, the expanded Barge Canal was used by bootleggers to move their products.

The canal didn't just have a tangential relationship to food through products and producers—there was a focus on cooking that traveled the length of the canal with innovative cooks and new recipes. Before the canal's completion, De Witt Clinton noted of one inn, "The swarms of flies which assailed the food, were very disgusting; and custards which were brought on the table, mal apropos exhibited of that insect as a substitute for the grating of nutmeg." Certainly not a five-star Yelp review. But that soon changed, as food preparation became an important feature of the canal's growth. As meals, just like alcohol, were considered

An 1825 image showing life on the locks. *NYPL Digital Collections.*

payment for services rendered, some contractors began hiring cooks. One that Pratt identified was Christine Davis, who cooked for canal workers with a seventeen-inch copper kettle, which she used throughout her tenure. The canal enabled cooks to feature ingredients they would not have had access to otherwise. Onetime luxury products like tea and coffee, sugar and pork were now commonplace.

One fun activity related to the canal, and one that can still be enjoyed today, was traveling the 363-mile waterway on a packet boat. These trips featured all-inclusive experiences in both dining and accommodations. The packet boats had large communal tables where guests would dine. After dinner, the tables were replaced by drop-down bedding for the night. Author Nathaniel Hawthorne would have given his journey an *A*, calling his meal on a packet boat "the pleasantest I had spent on the canal." Kate Lavender was one of the more colorful packet boat cooks. Using fine silver plates to serve her meals, Lavender, an English immigrant, was reputed to have a quick wit and some unconventional cooking methods. One was to place a cat on bread dough, as she maintained it helped the bread rise faster. Possibly again in the interest of speed, she was reputed to have baked her cherry pies pits and all. It's interesting to note that George Pullman, the inventor of the Pullman sleeping car and native of Brockton, New York,

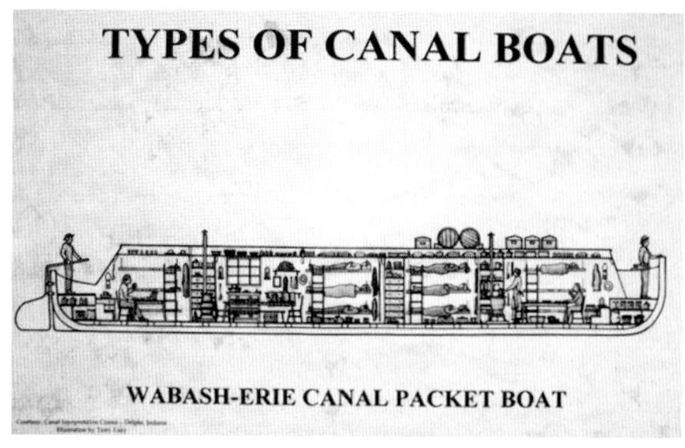

An inside look at a typical packet boat that traversed the canal. *Wikimedia Commons.*

was likely influenced by the packet boats. As the son of a carpenter who worked on the construction of the Erie Canal, Pullman was said to have been a passenger on an overnight trip originating in Buffalo. Unhappy with the cramped seats, he borrowed the packet boat concept of dining and sleeping to create a luxury experience. His sleeper cars were an instant hit. It was one of his designs that was part of the train carrying Lincoln's body back to Illinois. In a twist of fate, Lincoln's son Robert succeeded Pullman as president of the company.

Competition from the railways gave way to the enlargement of the canal to allow for barges to traverse the waterway. Several phases of expansion included adding locks as well as widening and deepening the actual trench to allow for larger vessels and the ability for two-way passage. The most significant overhaul came in 1907, when then Governor of New York Theodore Roosevelt began a full expansion to accommodate barges. Teddy's distant cousin Franklin Delano Roosevelt was said to have annually toured the canal system aboard a yacht named the *Inspector*. The meals aboard that vessel were served on fine dinnerware compliments of W.H. Farrar and the company he founded in 1841. Originally known as the Onondaga Pottery Company, it later became the Syracuse China Company, which sadly closed in 2009. The company, founded in Geddes, New York, was known for high-fired china much in demand on the high-end railway cars and barges. Just as packet boats elevated travel along the waterway, so did the barges on the newly expanded canal. Food naturally became an important feature of those journeys. One example was Oliver Wendell Petrie, born in 1899, in Oswego, New York. Petrie became a cook on the *Empire State*, an oil tanker that traversed the canal. While solidly preparing familiar dishes for the crew, Petrie dabbled in some more exotic dishes. He prepared everything from chile con carne to Hungarian goulash, and chop suey was a popular favorite in his repertoire. Erie Eats honors his legacy with a series of YouTube tutorials on some of his more popular dishes.

With the advent of refrigerated cars, foods not usually offered downstate became plentiful, and New York City was able to bring these products expeditiously and cheaply to a wider market. Towns sprang up along the course of the canal, and that brought with it employment, housing and restaurants, a newfangled concept to the area. One of the more well-known establishments for both lodging and dining was the Syracuse House. While it was known for its exemplary hospitality and delicious food, it has an interesting connection to New York's role in the Underground Railroad. Thomas Leonard, an African American man, was a waiter at the Syracuse House, and his wife, Jane, was a cook at the nearby Exchange Hotel. In 1839, the Davenports of Mississippi arrived at the Syracuse House with their domestic servant Harriet Powell. When local abolitionists learned of her arrival, it is rumored that they communicated with her through the Leonards, and she was whisked away to freedom across the border into Canada. Syracuse was a pivotal player in the Underground Railroad, and noted abolitionists Frederick Douglass and Harriet Tubman lived in nearby communities.

The connections between Upstate and progressive thinking abound. Elizabeth Smith Miller, daughter of abolitionist Gerrit Smith of Geneva, New York, is a great example. She was an outspoken voice for women's rights, joining forces with Stanton and Anthony in founding the National Woman Suffrage Association. Yet her 1875 cookbook *In the Kitchen* seems more of a how-to for the female homemaker than a forward-thinking treatise on women's rights. It is dedicated "respectfully to the 'Cooking Class of the Young Ladies Saturday Morning Club.'" She wrote of the virtues of maintaining a home through appropriate meals. The book contains over five hundred pages of international recipes reflecting the various immigrant groups that populated the Upstate region. Most remarkable is her treatise on the table. "No silent educator in the household has higher rank than the table. Surrounded three times a day by the family, who gather from their various callings and duties, eager for refreshment of the body and spirit." She implored the homemaker to place the breakfast table "in the centre of the room, and perfectly straight," for, "no matter how well arranged, if it stand but little out of line, everything looks awry." For dinner, she suggested starting with oysters, five or six at most, with a wedge of lemon, and should soup be served, "one ladleful and but one helping." Her best advice is how to enjoy a meal, suggesting a leisurely pace with "time to talk, laugh and be merry." Could Miller have been the first to articulate the slow food movement?

Progressive free thinker and author Elizabeth Smith Miller. *Courtesy of the Smith Miller NAWSA Scrapbooks.*

It would be remiss not to say that the canal, while a savior to Upstate farmers and merchants, was not a windfall for others. For the Haudenosaunee, the canal represented disruption and displacement, leaving profound effects on these first New Yorkers. Additionally, the rapid growth of the canal towns caused tremendous deforestation of the woodlands in Upstate New York, an environmental impact that was not a consideration at the time but had far-reaching ramifications. However, in total, it would seem, from a culinary standpoint, that it was a huge venture with great effect.

Today, tourists can still experience the Erie Canal in many unique ways. Visitors can rent houseboats and re-create the slow passage down the waterway, eating and sleeping aboard as travelers on packet boats did more than one hundred years before. You can rent kayaks to explore points of interest, and daily tour boats and charters are available for a leisurely informative tour. The trek allows visitors to view original buildings, such as the mills that were powered by the canal waters, and Lockport, home to the engineering feat of the "Flight of Five" locks in the Lockport Locks District (say that five times fast). More fun suggestions can be found in the "Where to Go" section at the back of the book.

• • • • • • • • •

Recipe: Nantucket Soup
Taken from In the Kitchen

½ pint codfish, picked fine
2 quarts water
3 ounces butter
1 ounce flour
½ teaspoon pepper
1 quart milk
3 eggs, beaten

Boil the codfish slowly in the water for 15 or 20 minutes, soften the butter with a little of the boiling water and mix it until smooth with the flour and pepper. Put it in the soup, and after boiling a minute or 2, add the milk. When it boils again, stir in the beaten eggs and serve with bread dice strewn over the top.

Chapter 5

HANGRY AT THE PAN

The first World's Fair I attended was held in 1964 in Flushing, Queens, about an hour's car ride from my home in Westchester. I was nine years old (you do the math), and I remember being floored by the enormity of the spectacle that my parents promised would be our best day

Nighttime photograph of the exposition with the electric tower in the background. *Library of Congress.*

ever. We were greeted by an awesome structure called the Unisphere, which conveyed the theme of this exposition, "Man's achievement on a shrinking globe in an expanding universe." I was a sophisticated child, having traveled extensively and dined in some of New York's best restaurants, yet I recall feeling overwhelmed by the scope of what I was encountering. Those feelings came flooding back to me as I delved into the 1901 Pan-American Exposition held in Buffalo, New York. How would a nine-year-old, who was possibly less savvy, view what she was witnessing? Would the spectacle of lights that emanated from the Electric Tower seem otherworldly? Would the masses of visitors crushing together to view the newest technology or invention seem daunting? Would the plethora of food choices from across the globe be boggling? The answer would have to be a resounding yes. The 1901 and 1964 fairs had much in common. They were both designed to showcase innovation, to bridge the gap between countries and cultures and to present their city in the best light possible.

Rainbow City

From May 1901 to November of that year, all eyes were on the Pan-American Exposition in Buffalo, New York. Some remember the event as a chance for the United States to share its progress in commerce and technology with the world. For most, however, it is remembered as the site where President William McKinley was assassinated. But when history looks back on the PAX, as those in the know call it, it was a triumph for Buffalo, New York State and America as a country. As Robert Rydell wrote in *All the World's a Fair*, the idea for the exposition was in the works for several years when in 1895 Buffalo railroad speculator John M. Brinker proposed at the American Exhibitor's Association that Buffalo was perfectly positioned to host. His case for Buffalo was an easy one to make. At the time, Buffalo was reachable for forty million people by a twelve-hour train ride. To sweeten the pot, he noted that Niagara Falls was not just a draw for tourists, but it could also provide the necessary electrical power to host a dazzling show of strength. In addition to the revenue the fair would generate and the prestige it would bring to Buffalo, it would also benefit neighboring towns and cities as hundreds of conventioneers flocked to the area, filling hotel rooms and taverns. It was a boon for the economy of Western New York. The organizers assembled an impressive array of team leaders to create what were called ethnological concessions, horticultural features, fountains, statues and architecture that screamed we are leading the way into the twentieth century!

The result was a flamboyant fair with blazing colors, stunning structures, a lively midway and an Electric Tower that cast an illuminating glow over the entire mall, rivaling Paris as the city of light. It was considered a climatic achievement, and the phallic imagery was not wasted on many. The tone was kaleidoscopic, as the fair was awash in color, earning Buffalo the nickname Rainbow City. The estimated eight million who came shelled out fifty cents per ticket, which gave them entrance to the exhibits and public spaces. There were exhibits reflective of the various countries present representing

Interior shot of the Niagara powerhouse, which electrified the exposition. *Library of Congress.*

not just Latin and North America but Native American offerings and American territories such as the Philippines. The buildings each focused on a singular discipline, including agriculture, machinery, horticulture and the arts. A main draw was the Manufactures and Liberal Arts Building, about which the *Official Catalogue and Guide to the Exposition* stated, "The visitor will find gathered in profusion the very latest productions of the mills and factories....Foods and their accessories...show the possibilities for food production."

This ticket allowed guests to enjoy all the exhibits, roam the midway and then purchase the food of their choice. *Wikimedia Commons, Pan-American Exposition Company, E.A. Wright, Banknote Engraver, Philadelphia.*

The exposition could be cynically viewed as one big advertisement disguised as a fun day at the fair. And as such you would expect corporations to tout their wares and accomplishments. Food-focused businesses were no exception. Companies such as Lowney's and Baker's Chocolate displayed and sold chocolates, bonbons and cocoa and attracted large crowds waiting to sample their products. Some other notable food companies that had exhibits included Borden's Condensed Milk, Heinz & Co., Pillsbury-Washburn Flour Mills, Saratoga Springs Mineral Water, Welches Grape-Juice Co. and Wesson Process Co. The Model Dairy was a way for New York to show off its dairy prowess, and the display maintained fifty cows that benefitted from the newest equipment. Their output was monitored daily, with all the milk and buttermilk they produced being distributed to visitors.

Months before the fair's opening, the *Pan-American Herald* discussed the food concessions. It was not a given that your concession would be granted space. Frederic Taylor, who was charged with the directorship of the Department of Concessions, entertained over two thousand applications before the exposition opened. Of all the concessions, Director Taylor put a premium on the food concessions. The *Herald* called restaurant permits "the greatest concession within the Exposition's gift." Taylor's aim was for the food service to be

> *a permanent advertisement for the Exposition and for Buffalo hospitality. The restaurants will be good. That will be insisted upon. The service must be above criticism. There will be various restaurants and various charges but each one must be as good as possible. If the charge for a meal is 50 cents the guest will be satisfied that he is getting as good a fifty cent meal as he can get in any restaurant or hotel in the land. If the meal is a dollar it must be correspondingly better.*

When asked if the main restaurant would be high class, he quipped, "higher than any restaurant in the United States in all probability as it may be located 120 feet above the ground in the Electric Tower." He then went on to compare its quality to New York City's Delmonico's and the famed Waldorf Astoria. He boasted, "The service will be perfect, the viands [an archaic term meaning an item of food] the richest, and the cooks and the waiters the best that money can secure." He encouraged those who could afford a splurge to bring a large party to celebrate what he called "gastronomic revelry." You could barely take a step without having something to eat or drink readily at hand. On her site "Doing the Pan," Susan Eck, a proud and prolific

The Pan-American Official Catalogue and Guide.

Dairy Building.

W. W. Hall, Supt.

EXHIBITORS.

De Laval Separator, 74 Cortlandt St., New York, N. Y. The De Laval cream separators are of the improved "Alpha" disc type and are as much superior to other separators as such machines are to gravity setting methods.

Heller and Merz, 55 Maiden Lane, New York, N. Y. Butter color.

Iron Clad Mfg. Co., 2-4-6 Cliff St., New York, N. Y. Cans and dairy supplies.

Oakes and Burger, Cattaraugus, N. Y. Cheese and butter factory supplies.

A. H. Reed, 30th & Market Sts., Philadelphia, Pa. Cream separator and pasteurizer.

C. T. Rogers and Son, Detroit, Mich. Milk condenser.

Sharples, P. M., West Chester, Pa. Tubular cream separators and supplies.

Star Milk Cooler Co., Haddonfield, N. J. Milk aerators.

Vermont Farm Machine Co., Bellows Falls, Vt. Separators and dairy apparatus. Improved U. S. cream separators and other dairy and creamery supplies.

LIVE STOCK PAVILION.

Allen Sheep Shearing Co., Chicago, Ill. Shearing machines.

Cornell Incubator Mfg. Co., Ithaca, N. Y. Incubators.

Columbia Incubator Co., Delaware City, Del. Incubators.

Holt, L. W., Rose Hill, N. Y. Automatic check.

Page, C. H., Buffalo, N. Y. Door guide and stay.

Cyphers Incubator Co., Wayland, N. Y. Incubators.

Anti-Cholera Co., Chicago, Ill. Medicines.

Marilla Incubator Co., Rose Hill, N. Y. Incubators.

Model Dairy.

Edward Van Alstyne, Supt.

In this department will be conducted a competitive test, lasting the entire six months during which the Exposition is open. Five head selected from each of the different breeds will participate.

THE ENTRY LIST IS AS FOLLOWS.

UNITED STATES.

American Devonshire Cattle Association.
American Guernsey Cattle Club.
Ayrshire Breeders' Association.
Brown Swiss Breeders' Association.
Dutch Belted Cattle Breeders' Association.
Red Polled Cattle Club of America.
American Polled Jersey Club.

CANADA.

Dominion Short Horn Breeders' Association.
Canadian Ayrshire Breeders' Association.
Canadian Jersey Cattle Association.
Canadian Holstein Friesien Association.
French-Canadian Cattle Breeders' Association.

126

In his description of the Dairy Hall, Superintendent Hall outlined the exhibitors and model dairy. *Library of Congress, official catalogue and guidebook to the Pan-American Exposition.*

Buffalo historian, shared some great info about the available food offerings. Eck reported that there were thirty-six restaurants with fifteen kitchens and fifty-seven soft drink stands. It is reported that water fountains also dotted the streets, making this the first venue to feature drinking fountains. As you would expect at a fair, the aim was to keep people moving, so most of the food establishments were grab-and-go.

The honor of occupying the tower's coveted spot went to Bailey's Catering Co., which had not one but nine restaurant concessions. The premier restaurant featured continental as well as familiar foods, and prices ranged from fifteen cents for radishes to sixty cents for a lobster salad. Offerings included sweetbreads glacé and Bluepoint oysters, which even by today's standards are quite cosmopolitan. Their Mirror Lake Pergola had a fairly short and simple menu with a few cold options such as salmon, capon and salami, as well as assorted sandwiches, deviled eggs and Buffalo beer in steins. If you were a member of the esteemed Foreign Commissioners, the Board of Directors would have hosted you to the gastronomic revelry Taylor described above. On June 29, attendees were treated to caviar canapés followed by Niagara bass in a meunière preparation, filet mignon and a dessert of mousse, gateaux and a gelée au champagne. It's curious to note that, to be deliberately pretentious, the menu was all in French.

Getting Hangry

The third-highest moneymaker was Alt Nürnberg, or "old Nürnberg," which was the creation of Jacob Schoellkopf and other wealthy German Americans. It was designed to recreate the beauty of their village back home. Lunchtime in an outdoor courtyard was reminiscent of an Oktoberfest gathering, as a forty-eight-piece German band and the Koenigseer troupe of singers and yodelers entertained guests as they dined. The pavilion featured a legendary restaurant named Lüchow's. Their traditional German food included wiener and paprika schnitzel, German pancakes, Westphalia ham and a vast selection of wines from the Rhine region. The most expensive item on the menu was a double sirloin with béarnaise sauce that would set you back $2.00 (which today would be equivalent to about $40.00). Both Alt Nürnberg and Pabst took a back seat to Bailey's, which brought in a gross revenue of $645,6017.13. Of these upscale options, Mary Bronson Hartt in a September 1901 article for *Everybody's Magazine* had these recommendations:

BAILEY CATERING CO.,

Pan Americna Exposition

Swift and Company's Meat Used Exclusively.

Thornton & Chesters Flour and Fleischmann &Co's Yeast Used Exclusively.

STADIUM | **Restaurant C.**

Bluepoints 30 Oyster Stew 30 Fried Oysters 40 Little Neck Clams 30

SOUP

English Beef Broth 30 Consomme, Caroline 25
Puree of Tomatoes, Caroline 30 Consomme Julienne 25
Consomme in Cup 20

RELISHES

Radishes 15 Cucumbers 25 Olives 25 Sliced Tomatoes 25
Chow Chow 15 Gherkins 15

FISH

Boiled Salmon, a l' Allemande 50 Broiled Whitefish, Hoteliere 45

BOILED

Ham with Cabbage 40

ENTREES

Sirloin of Beef, Stanley 75 Sweetbread Glace, Jardiniere 60
Chicken Croquettes, St Lambert 60 Green Apple Fritters, Rum Sauce 30

ROAST

Prime Ribs of Beef 45 Young Turkey Stuffed, with Currant Jelly 60

COLD

Roast Beef 45 Smoked Beef Tongue 40 Corned Beef 40
Swift's Premium Ham 40 Sardines (per box) 35 Spring Chicken, half 60

VEGETABLES

Boiled or Mashed Potatoes 15 Wax Beans 25
New Carrots in Cream 25 Butter Beets 20 Fried Egg Plant 20

SALADS

Chicken 60 Lobster 60 Potato 25 Lettuce 30

DESSERT

Cocoanut Pie 15 Apple Pie 10 Pie a la Mode 25
Vanilla Ice Cream 15 Chocolate Ice Cream 15 Assorted Cakes 20 Peaches and Cream 25
Watermelon 20 Canteloupe 25 American (Full Cream) Cheese 10
Edam 20 Swiss 20 Mac Larens Imperial Cheese 25 Neufchatel 20 Roquefort 25

DRINKS

"GREGG'S BRAND" MOCHA AND JAVA COFFEE, 10c cup Demi Tasse Coffee 10
Liptons Ceylon Tea (green) small pot 15 large pot 25
Liptons Ceylon Tea (black) small pot 15 large pot 25
Iced Tea 10 Iced Coffee 10 Cream (Glass(15 Milk (glass) 10 Cocoa 15 Chocolate 15
Apollinaris Splits 15, Pints 25 Quarts 40 Cantrell and Cochrane Belfast Ginger Ale 25
Cantrell and Cochrane Sarsaparilla 25 Cantrell and Cochrane Imported Club Soda 25
Vartray Ginger Ale 20 Crystal Syphons 20 Vartray Sarsaparilla 20
Norcross Aerated Buttermilk 10

........ONE PORTION SERVED TO TWO OR MOR 25c XTRA PR PLAT.........

Guests are requested to compare their checks with prices on this Bill

TUESDAY, SEPTEMBER. 3, 1901. [OVER]

Bailey Catering Company's main restaurant featured an array of continental offerings. *NYPL Digital Collections.*

If you are careless of expense it is easy to be happy; you dine in Alt Nurnberg, or up in the Tower....Habitues of the Exposition get their most substantial meal at noon at one of the cheaper places and sup lightly at Alt Nurnberg to the music of the fine band, or up on the colonnade of the Electric Tower with the whole sunlit spectacle spread out before them.

The Midway was the place to be when you were "hangry," providing a great option for those who preferred to wander into various concessions, like browsing the food court in your local mall. One of the most successful food ventures on the Midway was Pabst beer. They enticed visitors to imbibe by calling their beer "safer than water because it's always pure. Its nutrient properties maintain bodily vigor without taxing digestion, and there is just the mild stimulation necessary to refresh the weary." It also accounted for, according to Dr. Roswell Park, medical director of the exposition, only four cases of public intoxication, which is just one more than was suffered through electric shock and one less than syphilis! Pabst ran a successful venture, as it was one of the top three grossing concessions at the fair. Today we are accustomed to culturally diverse food, but back in 1901 it was an exotic selection. The goal of the exposition was to enlighten and expose visitors to people, places and things that were unfamiliar. Eck was quick to point out that when viewed with today's lens, some of these attempts were decidedly not in line with our current sensibilities. But for 1901, they thought they were being progressive and openminded.

Food representative of each country was offered at concessions such as Beautiful Orient, Fair Japan, Philippine Village, Venice in America and Streets of Cairo. One of the more popular was McGarvie's Streets of Mexico. There were toreadors and adobe huts, native dances and authentic music and, of course, traditional Mexican food. If you found yourself on the Streets of Mexico, you could have sampled tamales, chile con carne, salsa, enchiladas and frijoles. Meander a little further and you'd come across Mrs. McCready's Restaurant, where, the *Official Guide* said, "The visitor may procure foods of any description to satisfy 'the inner man.'" It was described as "a first-class restaurant in every particular and assured of a high-class patronage." You could always take a break from the food and see Esau, the educated chimpanzee who ate with a knife and fork, or Bonner, the educated horse, billed as "the wonderful talking-writing equine comedian, who is possessed of the intelligence almost human." It was said Bonner could perform simple math. The Midway was certainly not lacking for entertainment of all forms.

Pan-American Exposition
1901
BUFFALO, N. Y.

LÜCHOW'S PAN-AMERICAN RESTAURANT CO.,

German Village, Alt Nürnberg.

F. A. WAHL, Manager.

AUGUST LÜCHOW, 108-114 East 14th Street, New York.

SOLE AGENT FOR THE UNITED STATES

Wurzburger Hofbrau, Brauhaus Wurzburg.

Original Pilsner, Pilsner Genossenschafts Brauerei.

The celebrated WURZBURGER HOFBRAU and ORIGINAL PILSNER can be bought in Bottles for Family Use, Clubs and Restaurants, through

C. PERSONS' SONS, 390-392 Elm Street, BUFFALO, N. Y.

Lüchow's German-inspired menu at Alt Nürnberg. *NYPL Digital Collections.*

Above: Elaborate buildings and what was then considered politically correct costuming marked the exhibits dotting the midway. *Library of Congress, The Pan-American and Its Midway.*

Right: People dressed in authentic clothing from the country they represent help greet diners to their pavilion. *Library of Congress, The Pan-American and Its Midway.*

Sept. 4, 1901.

BILL OF FARE.

Streets of Mexico Restaurant,

PAN-AMERICAN EXPOSITION, BUFFALO, N. Y.

H. F. McGARVIE, Concessionaire. — 1901. — B. F. LOCKE, Manager.

Mexican Tamales,	25 cts.	Mexican Enchiladas,	25 cts.
Mexican Chile Con Carne,	~~15~~ " 25	Mexican Frijoles,	~~5~~ " 25
Mexican Salsa,	~~15~~ " 25		

SOUPS

Consomme,	15 cts.	Consomme with Rice,	20 cts.
Tomato,	~~15~~ " 20	Bisque of Tomato,	20 "

FISH (in season).

Fresh Perch,	30 cts.	Blue Fish,	30 cts.	Fresh Mackerel,	30 "
Yellow Pike,	30 "	White Fish,	30 "		

Ex Sirloin Steak 60

STEAK, CHOPS. Etc.

Small Sirloin Steak,	45 cts.	Extra Large Porterhouse Steak,	$1.50
" Tenderloin "	50 "	Hamburg Steak,	25 cts.
" Porterhouse "	65 "	Lamb Chops,	40 "
~~Extra Single Porterhouse Steak,~~	80 "	Veal Steak,	50 "
Medium " "	90 "	" Chops,	40 "
Pork Chops,	40 "	Ham fried or broiled,	50 "

POTATOES, VEGETABLES.

Potatoes German Fried,	10 cts.	Stewed Corn,	10 cts.
" Hashed Brown,	10 "	" Tomatoes,	10 "
" Stewed,	10 "	String Beans,	10 "
" Lyonnaise,	10 "	French Peas,	20 "
" French Fried,	10 "	" Mushrooms,	25 "
" Saratoga,	10 "	Fried Onions,	10 "
" Julienne,	15 "		

SPECIAL DISHES TO-DAY.

SALADS, RELISHES.

Sliced Tomatoes,	15 cts.	Lettuce,	15 cts.
" Cucumbers,	20 "	Lettuce and Tomatoes,	25 "
" Tomatoes and Onions,	15 "	Lettuce with Mayonnaise,	20 "
Welsh Rarebit,	40 "	Yorkshire Buck,	50 "
Golden Buck,	50 "		

EGGS.

Boiled Eggs,	20 cts.	Plain Omelette,	25 cts.	Ham and Eggs,	40 cts.
Fried "	20 "	Ham "	25 "	Bacon " "	35 "
Poached "	20 "	Parsley "	25 "	Scrambled Eggs,	20 "

TOAST, Etc.

Dry Toast,	5 cts.	French Toast,	20 cts.	Cream Toast,	25 cts.
Buttered Toast,	10 "	Milk Toast,	15 "		

COLD DISHES.

Roast Beef, with Potato Salad,	40 cts.	Imported Swiss Cheese Sandwich,	15 cts.
Ham, with Potato Salad,	40 "	Sardine Sandwich,	15 "
Ham Sandwiches,	10 "	" Box (imported),	25 "
Imported Swiss Cheese, with Crackers,	25 "		

Coffee, with Cream, per cup,	10 cts.	Tea, with Cream, per cup,	10 cts.
" " " " pot,	15 "	" " " " pot,	15 "
Milk, per glass,	10 "	Milk and Cream, " glass,	15 "
		Cream, per glass,	20 "

MEXICAN CHILE SAUCES WILL BE SERVED WITH THE ABOVE DISHES, IF DESIRED.

Bread and Butter 10 cts. extra with all orders of less than 25 cts.

The Streets of Mexico rang out with mariachi music and authentic food. *NYPL Digital Collections.*

READ ALL ABOUT IT

For the cost-conscious, Hartt had this to say: "Sandwiches and such unstaying [*sic*] trifles can be had at lunch counters everywhere, but they are not cheaper than more substantial dishes—that is, if you buy enough to sustain life." If there was no room at the counter, fairgoers needn't worry, as there were reportedly eighteen thousand park bench seats that lined the fairgrounds. For those truly on the run, vendors who strolled the grounds and stationary kiosks sold familiar foods such as chowder and beans, fruit, peanuts and, of course, ice cream. There were two great options for the truly frugal. They could bring boxed lunches to be enjoyed under a shady tree near the Delaware Park entrance or seated on one of those eighteen thousand bench spaces. The lunches for some had to withstand lengthy travel or a twelve-hour train ride, and many who came from out of state brought their lunches to their state's pavilion and then visited it later in the day to be enjoyed. Not sure how well macaroni salad or cobbler would do in the sweltering

Three ladies of leisure enjoy people watching on one of the thousands of benches strewn throughout the expo. *Library of Congress, Johnston, Frances Benjamin.*

heat of a July day, but boxed lunches were so popular that it was said there was an ocean of litter from the several thousand shoeboxes used to hold the lunches. Lavinia Hart described the lunches at the Manufactures and Liberal Arts Building pavilion in an article she wrote for *Cosmopolitan* in September 1901. Touring there, one could eat their way through the exhibits without spending a dime, much like a trip to Costco munching free samples as you wander down the aisles.

> *All types of women were huddled together, rich and poor, esthetic and commonplace. It was lunch-time* [sic], *and they were engaged in the work of managing a free lunch. Women whose diamonds were gems and whose gowns were creations elbowed women who might have been their cooks, to get free biscuit made from the "finest baking powder on earth;" free pancakes made from the only pancake flour that wouldn't result in sinkers; free soup from the only cans containing real tomatoes; free samples of all the varieties of mustard, jam and pickles; free sandwiches of minced meat; free cheese, preserves, chow-chow, plum pudding, clam broth, baked beans and pickled lobster.*

Written with disarming wit, Mrs. L.O. Harris in an article for the *Boston Cooking School Magazine* gave some humorous insights into the food at the fair. Her first related to the educational factors and reflected the accepted wisdom of the day. "What nobler occupation for her activities can a young woman find than the mastery of the art of human brain, bone and muscle building?...The modern foodshow [*sic*] rises to a dignity above the mere purposes of trade, when it inspires and helps womankind to this end." She touted the sophisticated palate that would welcome new tastes, such as yerba maté made from a South American shrub or tania, a tuber that is sweet and white. She reviewed mandioc derived from the cassava plant and popular in Argentina and questioned whether North American cooks truly knew how to use peppers. Harris recommended a Chilean food called alimento klein, a composite of milk, cocoa and other unnamed nutrients that she felt was suitable for "infants, invalids and old people." She hinted at some new food inventions such as instant coffee (which she found distasteful) and onion and celery salt, which she applauded. Of the bread offerings, she suggested, "When bread was declared to be the staff of life, the human stomach must have been made of sterner stuff." Calling these carbs the "bread of affliction," could she have been an early proponent of the low carb diet? Continuing her diatribe about the awful offerings and newfangled items, she declared that "American stomachs have gone on strike." However, she did find some things useful, one being baking powder made from the whites of eggs and Aunt Jemima (now branded as Pearl Milling) pancakes made from a new processed flour. She was a fan of Florida and California's entries of pawpaw juice, which tenderized meat; the Japan plum and loquat fruit, which she described as having an acidic but sweet flavor; and the olives, prunes, raisins and almonds, which she felt were superior to those that were imported. Her summary was an overall mixed bag, but it provides insight into how these new food introductions were viewed by someone well-versed in the culinary world at that moment in time.

The burning question for any attendee at the Exposition was, where are the pies? The *Buffalo Evening News* answered that crucial question in a March 7, 1901 article. The headline of the article promised that the building where the pies were to be baked would be immense, and the kitchen being constructed would prepare food for millions.

VENICE IN AMERICA

The Venice exhibit was replete with pigeons flown in to recreate the atmosphere in St. Mark's Square. *Library of Congress, The Pan American and Its Midway.*

The Pan-American Official Catalogue and Guide.

Department of Foods and Their Accessories.

FREDERIC W. TAYLOR, Sup't.

EXHIBITORS.

Akron Cereal Co., The, Akron, O. D—49.

American Cereal Co., The, 90 W. Broadway, New York. D—42.

Armsby, J. K. Co., 44 River St., Chicago, Ill. F—49.

Arethusa Spring Water Co., Seymour, Conn. D—36.

Armour & Co., 205 La Salle St., Chicago, Ill. D—45.

Borden's Condensed Milk Co., 71 Hudson St., New York, N. Y. A—46.

Consumers' Company, The, 35th and Butler Sts. ,Chicago, Ill. C—46.

Davis Milling Co., R. T., St. Joseph, Mo. C—37.

Dold Packing Co., Jacob, Buffalo, N. Y. F—51.

Erie Preserving Co., Buffalo, N. Y. C—44.

Egg Baking Powder Co., 80 West St., New York. D—48.

Fairbank Co., N. K. The, 277 Dearborn St., Chicago, Ill. G—29.

Fisher & Co., B., 397 Greenwich St., New York, care C. D. Petrie, Buffalo, N. Y. D—40.

German-American Provision Co., The, Union Stock Yards, Chicago, Ill. G—46.

Exhibit of Blue Ribbon Brand Canned Meats, fancy sausages and cream table lard.

Geneva Mineral Water Co., Brooklyn, N. Y. B—44. Geneva Mineral (Lithia) Water as produced in nature's laboratory. Buffalo's depot, 50 W. Eagle St. Main office, 20 Court St., Brooklyn, N. Y. Perfectly pure. Pleasantly practical. Pan-American peoples know its virtues and profit by them. See our exhibit. Try a sample and get some interesting information and a beautiful souvenir.

Heide, Henry, 84 Vandam St., New York, N. Y. C—49.

Heinz Co., H. J., Pittsburg, Pa. C—36.

Heekin & Co., James, Walnut and Water Sts., Cincinnati, O. E—48.

Hecker-Jones-Jewell Milling Co., New York City. C—49.

Hickmott Asparagus Canning Co., San Francisco, Cal. D—36.

Horlick's Food Co., Racine, Wis. ·B—48.

Hotaling-Warner Co., Syracuse, N. Y. A—47.

Imperial Granum Co., 153 Water St., New York. F—46.

Knox, Charles, Johnstown, N. Y. F—42.

Kato Coffee Co., 509 Monadnock Bldg., Chicago, Ill.

Klinck, C., Buffalo, N. Y. D.—46.

Lackawanna Dairy Co., The, Scranton, Pa. D—39.

Libby, McNeill & Libby, Chicago, Ill. H—45.

MacLaren Imperial Cheese Co., A. F., Toronto, Ont. B—48.

Mohican Spring Water Co., Newark, N. J. D—51.

McCready, Mrs. J. C., 45 E. Utica St., Buffalo, N. Y. B—51.

Mellins Food, Boston, Mass. F—44

Nelson Morris Co., The, Union Stock Yards, Chicago, Ill. B—42.

Chicago, E. St. Louis, St. Joseph. Beef and pork packers, lard and oil refiners; mutton, canned meats, sausage, beef extract, fertilizers, etc. This booth exhibits the multitudinous products of this huge packing concern.

Nestle, Henry, 73 William St., New York. C—39.

National Food Co., H. D. Perky, Trustee, Worcester, Mass. A—44.

85

This page and opposite: Compiled by the superintendent of the expo, these pages show the variety of food companies represented at the expo. *Library of Congress, official catalogue and guidebook to the Pan-American Exposition.*

Oneida Community Co., The, Niagara Falls, N. Y. C—51.

Oscar Co., The, 105 Hudson St., New York. A—48.

Patent Cereal Co., Henry A. Davis, Utica, N. Y. E—42.

Pillsbury-Washburn Flour Mills Co., Minneapolis, Minn. A—38.

Runkel Bros., 445 W. 30th St., New York, N. Y. C—48.

Swift & Co., Union Stock Yards, Chicago, Ill. G—46.

St. Charles Condensing Co., St. Charles, Ill. B—49.

Sauer Co., C. F., The, Richmond, Va. B—51.

Smith, Kline & French Co., Canal and Poplar Sts., Philadelphia, Pa. D—47.

Washburn-Crosby Co., The, 644 Prudential Bldg., Buffalo, N. Y. C—38.

Wesson Process Co., The, Philadelphia, Pa. G—42.

Welch Grape-Juice Co., The, Westfield, N. Y. E—51.

> *The plan is to have the kitchen apart from the restaurants which it will purvey in order that the odors of the flower beds may have a chance against the redolent tornadoes of cooking smells that are bound to escape from the pie foundry...with a capacity of 50,000 of these pastries every day, and which will enthrone Buffalo, for one season at least, as Queen of the Pie Belt.*

The article decided that for its sheer grand size alone, Kitchen had earned its capital *K*. Estimated to be 200 feet long, 150 feet deep and two stories high, it would be utilized exclusively for cooking and baking except for rooms set aside for the chef and scullions (an archaic term for a servant designated to do menial tasks). The building would be designed with windows on the first floor that would allow visitors to watch "the wondrous transformation of strange substances into mince pie." Their ingenuity surfaced in addressing the issue of how to get hot food to restaurants that could be up to one mile away. They devised a system of overhead trolley lines, with large baskets

Stereograph from 1901 as McKinley addressed fairgoers. *NYPL Digital Collections.*

mounted on the trolley wheels. Their chief concern was the ravenous birds who could intercept the food en route, noting that they anticipated the arrival of five hundred pigeons from Venice. The medical director, Dr. Park, reported health concerns from soiled food and unsanitary conditions in a summary published after the fair closed. There were two thousand guests treated for digestive issues and one death from ptomaine poisoning (fair organizers maintained it was not contracted at the fair). Many concessions were cited for improper food handling or unsafe conditions, and one candy concession was closed down because the fair organizers found a family of four sleeping under the counter where they lived, cooked and ate. But as a whole and considering the huge attendance, the instances of food-related illnesses were relatively low and the infractions minor.

While the exposition was certainly marred by McKinley's assassination on September 5 at the Temple of Music, it did regain momentum and ran as promised until the start of November. It is interesting to note that Dr. Park was later maligned, as he was not on the grounds of the exposition on the day McKinley was shot. The story, as reported by Sally Ryan Costik for the Bradford Landmark Society, stated that after the shooting, a messenger was sent to Niagara Falls, where Park was performing surgery. Park responded, saying, "Can't you see that I can't leave this case, not even if it were for the president of the United States." The messenger then replied, "Doctor, it is for the president of the United States." Upon completing the procedure, Park was taken by train to the hospital setup at the exposition, finding that in his absence the only doctor on duty was a gynecologist. It has been implied that if Park had been available, McKinley might have survived, and Teddy Roosevelt would not have been sworn in.

Chapter 6

UDDERLY UPSTATE

If you're too young to remember Elsie the cow, I apologize for the anachronistic reference. For those of us who are familiar with Borden's mascot, you might recall that she was the symbol of the happy, pure, perfect bovine who produced dairy products above reproach. Elsie felt right at home in Upstate New York alongside hundreds of thousands of less famous milking cows. In Wassaic, New York, Borden, the company that anointed her, commercialized the first condensed milk, nourished the Union army and revolutionized the industry with glass bottles. That's just a drop in the milk pail of dairy's illustrious history in Upstate New York.

For more than four hundred years, the bucolic topography of the region has made it hospitable for cows to graze. It might sound udderly impossible to believe, but according to a 2020 survey by the New York State Dairy Statistics, there are 625,000 cows in Upstate New York, which is three times the population of Syracuse. The dairy industry of New York, with 90 percent of it located in the Upstate region, produces a staggering array of dairy products. I'm a sucker for statistics because numbers don't lie. In a quick-fire round of stats, those 625,000 cows found on 3,600 farms produce more than 15 billion pounds of milk annually. Wyoming County has the most cows at 47,000, with Cayuga a close second. This makes the dairy industry the state's most remarkable success story, ranking it fourth in the country. It is interesting to note that 99 percent of all milk, cream and skim used in dairy across the country comes from Upstate New York. These cows help produce 144 million pounds of cottage cheese, the most in the country.

Borden ads featured Elsie the cow prominently, and she remained an advertising icon for decades. *Wikimedia Commons.*

New York produces the most cream cheese as well, producing 294 million pounds, and leads the production of sour cream and yogurt. For the lactose intolerant, it might make living in New York precarious, but for anyone who loves a schmear of cream cheese on their bagel, sour cream topping their overstuffed potato or a yogurt parfait, it's a win. Milk might not be the sexiest topic to cover; perhaps the milky mustache it can produce is a mood killer. But it's important to note that without this pure milk, we would not have the excellent cheese and dairy products that New York is known for.

SAY CHEESE

There's a lot of Upstate history behind one of the most popular foods this side of France. Many might think of Wisconsin when you hear the word *cheese*, but you would be just as accurate if you said Herkimer County, New York. Eric Brunger, in his article detailing the growth of the New York State Dairy Industry for a journal called *New York History*, noted that from the period of 1850 to 1900, New York was the leading cheese producer, at times making quadruple the amount of its nearest competitor. We're talking close to 600 million pounds during this time frame. While it certainly didn't invent the art of cheesemaking, Herkimer County had a big slice of the market. In a country ripe with expertise, cheesemaking was practiced by many early settlers, notably the Dutch and Germans. But it took Herkimer County and others in the surrounding area to bring cheesemaking to the next level and put New York on the cheesemaking map.

With wine, it's all about the grape; for dairy, it's all about the cow, or so said dairy expert Xerxes Addison Willard in his *Dairy Farming* report dated 1862. The study focused on Herkimer County, located just north of the Mohawk River. It's home to quaint towns like Little Falls and historic sites such as Shoemaker Tavern, where George Washington didn't sleep but did enjoy a meal under a large shade tree. Willard's treatise guided the dairymen of Upstate New York on how to raise the best cows to obtain the best milk to create the best cheese. As Willard said, "It costs as much to keep a poor cow as it does a good, and that no more." So, he urged the dairyman to make suitable investments in his pastures and the seeds used to grow the grass that feeds the cow.

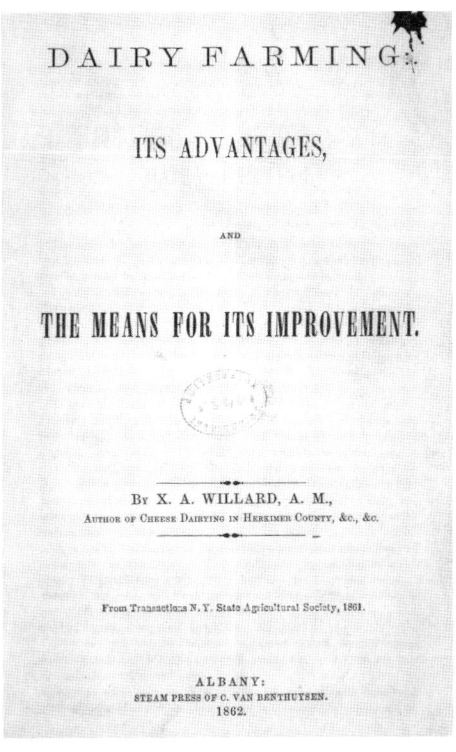
DAIRY FARMING:

ITS ADVANTAGES,

AND

THE MEANS FOR ITS IMPROVEMENT.

BY X. A. WILLARD, A. M.,
AUTHOR OF CHEESE DAIRYING IN HERKIMER COUNTY, &c., &c.

From Transactions N. Y. State Agricultural Society, 1861.

ALBANY:
STEAM PRESS OF C. VAN BENTHUYSEN.
1862.

The 1862 handbook for Herkimer County dairy farming written by Xerxes Addison Willard. *Library of Congress.*

He described the right kind of building to age and store the cheese and the exact equipment needed to prepare it from start to finish. Imagine the painstaking research involved for someone to write on the dangers of too many daisies in a field, but that's just what Willard did when he wrote, "Daisy pastures give a bitter taint to milk, which is perceptible in the cheese." His devotion to the topic and contribution to the art of dairy farming in New York is unmatched.

For the better part of the nineteenth century, counties in the Mohawk Valley of New York, most notably Chenango and Herkimer, were the hubs of the cheese wheel. Since they first arrived, settlers in many colonies were producing credible Cheddar and Cheshire cheese long before the country became a country. Not so, countered B.D. Gilbert, who carried a job title that sounds like it came from the *X-Files*, "Special Expert Agent Dairy Division." According to an 1896 report on the cheese industry by the State of New York, he reported the product was substandard. He referenced one taste tester, who asked, "Why is it that while tons of this article [cheese] are brought to our market [Albany] it is so extremely difficult to find any which a man of taste would tolerate on his table?" That soon changed.

Enter Jonathan Burrell, whom the Little Falls Historical Society credits as the leading businessman in the area for dairy products. The Burrells represented local dairymen as they peddled their collective dairy products in the fall of each year. When Jonathan died, his son Harry continued in the business in Salisbury, just six miles north of Little Falls. The local business gave way to a New York City–based cheese brokerage, and they became the first merchants to ship cheese to Philadelphia and as far as England. Their influence was so profound that the cheese exported from Upstate to England was being sold for gold, actually influencing the gold and sterling exchange. However, the cheese produced in New York we called Cheddar was disparagingly termed "American cheese" or "Yankee cheese" by the Brits. Harry's death led to a local scandal of sorts when in 1879, the vault where he was interred was broken into and his remains stolen. Two weeks later, they were recovered, and he was reinterred. The four robbers each received five-year sentences of hard labor in a prison located in Auburn, New York. That'll teach them to mess with the "big cheese."

At the same time Burrell was shifting the dynamics of the dairy business came a dairyman from Rome, New York, who brought the cheese industry into the nineteenth century. The Williams family had been farming the area since the Revolutionary War. Culturecheesemag.com noted that Jesse Williams and his wife were the owners of "265 acres of improved land, 65

This image, titled *Souvenir of Rome*, shows Jesse Williams and his cheese factory in 1894. *Library of Congress, Ninde, William E.*

head of cattle, 3 horses, 72 sheep, 27 hogs, 30 yards of fulled cloth and 40 yards of flannel." They certainly would have given the Duttons of TV's Yellowstone Ranch a run for their money. They had their hand in raising crops and livestock as well as operating a gristmill and country store. While other family members focused on wheat, Williams turned his attention to cheesemaking. In their report *Farm and Factory: Agricultural Production Strategies and the Cheese and Butter Industry*, authors Gibb, Bernstein and Zipp discussed Williams's endeavors in great detail. They cited an 1864 report in the *Utica Morning Herald* that credited Williams with the invention of "associated dairying." Williams was the first to develop a strategy to produce cheese by centralizing production. He took the milk from nearby farms, combined it with his and opened what could be called the first cheese factory in 1851. Culturecheesemag.com noted that Jesse and his equally impressive wife, Amanda, purportedly surveyed farms across Upstate New York to learn best practices from cultivators in Oneida, Otsego, Lewis and Herkimer. Their goal was not to simply produce more cheese but to produce the best cheese.

Jesse Williams's biographer Frederick A. Rahmer called him "by far the best cheesemaker in this country and perhaps the world." Jesse was considered the premier centralized cheesemaker, and he imparted his wisdom freely, resulting in five hundred similar cheese factories sprouting up in the area. In its first season, the Williams Cheese Factory produced upward of 100,000 pounds of cheese, utilizing the milk of three to four hundred cows. On the centennial of Jesse's creation of the cheese factory system, the city of Rome held a celebration attended by John H. Kraft, the president of Kraft Foods. He praised Jesse, calling him a trailblazer who helped make America great and added, "Where would our nation be had not pioneers such as Jesse dared to do things differently?"

In no way meant to diminish or discredit Jesse Williams, the town of Cuba, New York, offers a slightly different nibble concerning the first true cheese factory. The Cuba Cheese Shoppe noted that during the 1800s, the local farmers brought their cheese to a central location in Cuba, a town located in Allegheny County in Western New York. The cheese was then brought to New York City and sold at a price that was fixed weekly when the cheesemongers met at the Kinney Hotel in downtown Cuba. In 1871, twenty years after the Williams family established their cheese factory, Hosea and Andrew Ackerly, along with partner Daniel Sill, formed the first cheese company in Cuba. Maybe it could just be the nuance of the words *factory* versus *company* that causes the divergent stories.

Cheesemaking did more than just enrich the dairy farmers. It gave way to other industries, as the buildings that were needed to process the cheese had exact specifications, which in turn necessitated local carpenters to construct the facilities. Those in Utica and Rome especially benefitted by providing vats, presses, thermometers and scales. The cheese factories now dotted the Upstate landscape and stood out, unlike needles in the proverbial haystack, standing two and three stories high with billowing smokestacks.

Cheddar and hard cheeses were not the only types being produced in the area. In a section called "Fancy Cheese," the 1896 report cited cream cheese, pineapple cheese, Limburger, domestic Swiss and Müenster, among the others made in Upstate New York. One of those "fancy cheeses" is best known for being one part of the Sunday brunch triumvirate: lox, bagels and a schmear of cream cheese. In 1880, businessman C.D. Reynolds partnered with W.A. Lawrence of Chester, New York, to produce cream cheese. As I wrote in my book *Iconic New York Jewish Food*, Lawrence stumbled on cream cheese by adding too much heavy cream while trying to replicate Neufchâtel, a soft French cheese. Reynolds established a factory through

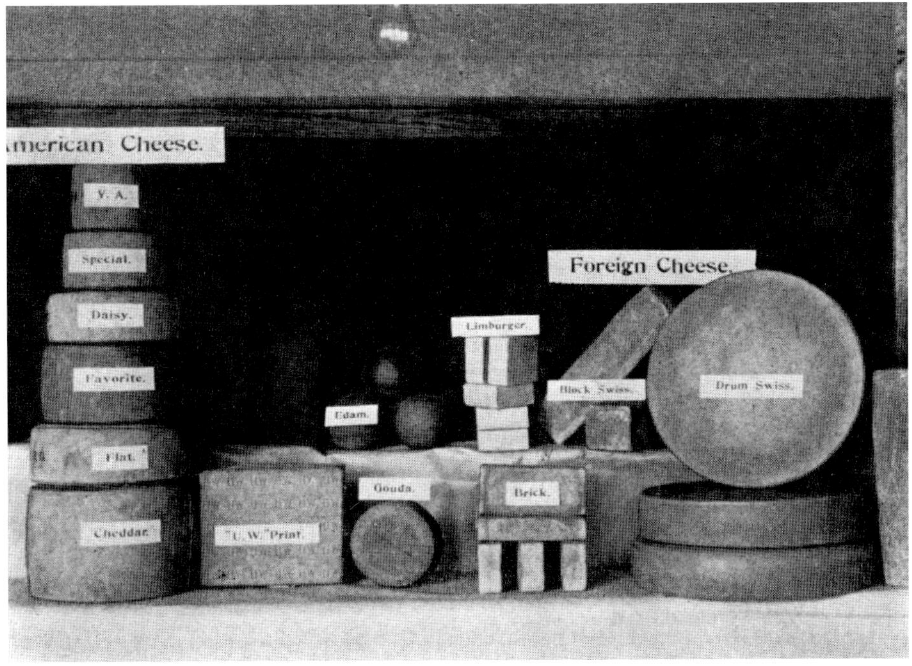

The Mohawk Book Company based in Little Falls published this image of the "fancy cheeses" that the region was producing. *Library of Congress, Frederikson, Johan Ditlev.*

the Empire Cheese Company (which coincidentally purchased the Cuba Cheese plant) in South Edmeston, New York. He rebranded the cream cheese "Philadelphia," not because of any affiliation with the city but, some suspect, because the city had an upscale urbane appeal and he wanted to gentrify his product. Empire's facility suffered a great fire that destroyed the factory and gave way to a company called Phenix, as the name connoted a factory that rose from the ashes, albeit incorrectly spelled. In 1928, Phenix was purchased by J.L. Kraft, which brought the product and its company to national recognition. And if creating cream cheese is not enough glory for Upstate cheesemakers, Velveeta Cheese is also an Upstate innovation. Natasha Geiling, who wrote about the cheese for a 2014 article in *Smithsonian Magazine*, said that in 1918, Emil Frey, who worked at the Monroe Cheese Company in Monroe, New York, created the processed product as a way to salvage cheese tidbits that were the by-product of the manufacturing process. They chose the name Velveeta, which evokes a "velvety smooth" food. Kraft Foods, which bought the company in 1927, slightly disputes this version, citing they based Velveeta on their recipe, not Frey's.

The Science of Dairying

At the same time that dairy farmers were making improvements and advances in their fields, researchers and scientists were hard at work providing scholarly information to aid in their growth. It was in June 1880 that the New York Agricultural Experiment Station was authorized. While not the first in the country, this experiment station, instead of exploring UFOs and unraveling the mysteries of cloning, focused on how to elevate and improve agricultural outcomes. The station was established in Geneva, New York, with the goal, as stated by its first director, E. Lewis Sturtevant, to "assert the best efforts, through research and science to improve the outcomes for dairy and agriculture in the area." They were headquartered in an Italian villa on a parcel of about 130 acres known as Parrott Hall. The station continued to expand and, by the turn of the century, had nine divisions, including agronomy, animal husbandry, dairying and horticulture. One of the challenges the station encountered was to get farmers to heed their advice. Many preferred the traditional methods of farming and dairy, avoiding what they termed "book farming." In the 1899 annual report, Director I.P. Roberts noted that many of the farmers they were trying to educate were "largely composed of those who had passed the youthful

Parrott Hall, where the New York Agricultural Experiment Station was first located, in 1900. *Wikimedia Commons.*

period of life, when courage, hope and vigor are at their best." Their research was very in-depth in matters that were practical and relevant to the dairy farming industry, from a study of "the period of gestation in cows" to "ropiness in milk and cream." H.H. Wing, the director of dairy husbandry, noted that local dairy schools were providing instruction in the best practices for butter and cheese making, with local creameries and cheese factories seeking their instruction. This receptive nature to what the station was accomplishing was indicated by the director commenting that "the farmers are now in a receptive mood." And posting one farmer's comment: "When I was at Cornell, many years ago, agriculture had no charms for me; now I would gladly exchange some of my living and dead languages, mathematics, etc., for a knowledge of dairying." In 1923, the station became part of Cornell University College of Agriculture Life Sciences, known now as AgriTech, and has helped shape the advances and possibilities for New York State in ways that the dairy farmers in the 1800s could never have imagined.

Butter

A sample SAT analogy question might be: Cheese is to Herkimer County as Butter is to _____? The answer would be Orange County, which churned out tons of butter during the heyday of Upstate dairy farming. "Goshen butter," as it was known, became a national commodity in the 1830s. We have entered a gray geographic area, as some might feel I am bending the boundaries of Upstate by including Goshen, but I feel it is well worth ticking off the geography buffs to share this information. Neversinkmuseum.org reported that a group of dairy farmers in Orange County all agreed to send their butter to New York City each year on the second Tuesday in November. The butter was stored in firkins, a type of wood cask, which would then make the long trek from Goshen to Albany via large wagons and barges that were towed by steamboats down the Hudson River. So vital was Goshen butter to the local economy that the National Bank of Orange County, which the museum reported was "one of the nation's wealthiest local corporations at the time," used yellow paper to print its currency as a homage to the butter industry. The first true butter factory was built in 1856 and was named Campbell Hall. It relied on the nearby cold springs to chill the butter, as refrigeration had not yet been invented. The railroads were

This road marker created in 1956 pays tribute to Campbell Hall, the location of the first true American butter factory. *Wikimedia Commons, Doug Kerr.*

a blessing and a curse for some Upstate businesses; for butter it proved the latter. Fluid milk could now be transported quickly and easily, causing the butter industry to wane.

YOGURT

No discussion of New York's impact on the dairy industry would be complete without a conversation about yogurt. Yogurt has been a food fad since the time of Neolithic man. I wrote an entire book on the subject, but I will fast-forward several thousand years to take us from Anatolia (Turkey) to Upstate New York's role in yogurt production. Suffice it to say that yogurt was not a new phenomenon; however, the type of yogurt that put Upstate New York on the map was. As yogurt made its way into the trend to eat healthy, brands such as Dannon and Yoplait dominated the American markets. That was until a Turkish-Kurdish–born entrepreneur named Hamdi Ulukaya entered the scene. Eyeing a plant in South Edmeston (yes, the same town that gave birth to cream cheese), Ulukaya brought his love for yogurt to Upstate New York. He also brought a yogurt master from his homeland, and together they tested various strains and different techniques and developed a thick strained Greek yogurt that we know today as Chobani. The name harkens back to the Turkish word for "shepherd," and Ulukaya definitely shepherded in a new era in yogurt production. Chobani, along with Fage, another Greek-styled yogurt, has launched Upstate New York as the leading producer of yogurt in the country, turning out more Greek-styled yogurt than Greece! Chobani joins companies such as Fage in Johnstown, Siggi's in Penn Yan, Alpina in Batavia, Agrana in Central New York and Sunrise located in the Southern Tier in establishing Upstate as the yogurt center of the nation. From goat's milk to sheep and cow's milk, yogurt is so integral to New York's economy that in 2014, Governor Andrew Cuomo designated yogurt as the state's official snack.

Ice Scream, You Scream, We All Scream

If you had asked me what one of my biggest wishes for this book was, I'd say crediting Upstate New York with inventing ice cream. Unfortunately, not all wishes are granted, so I'll have to settle for a bit of disputed food lore. The well-documented but unconfirmed story goes that perhaps the first ice cream sundae was created in Ithaca, New York. Food historian Andrew F. Smith wrote that clergy in the 1890s began to question if there was something unholy about drinking an ice cream soda on a Sunday. It was seen as a frivolous activity that should be avoided on the Sabbath. From this pious objection, the practice of eating rather than drinking ice cream became the trend. Enter the Reverend John Scott, who, as reported by WhatsCookingAmerica.net, entered Platt & Colt Pharmacy on April 3, 1892, in Ithaca's downtown. There he and the shop's owner, Chester C. Platt, engaged in conversation over a bowl of ice cream that fountain clerk Deforest Christiance prepared. Platt instructed his counterman to embellish the usual scoop of vanilla ice cream by topping it with cherry syrup and a candied cherry on top. In her blog, "Heather on History," Heather Voight expanded this version of the sundae's creation by highlighting the work of some Ithaca high school students. They searched the ledger books of the pharmacy and found that Platt had on hand those ingredients used for the sundae. They also discovered that in an article dated two days later in the *Ithaca Daily Journal*, the very same sundae was advertised. At the time, it was referred to as a "cherry Sunday," but some posit that the spelling was changed so as not to offend churchgoers and imply that this confection had anything to do with the Sabbath. Further documents show the pharmacy in 1894 applied for a trademark on the name "ice cream sundae," which some feel further cements their ties to the original dish. In 1936, Christiance wrote in a letter,

> *About the much discussed origin of the ice cream concoction called Sunday, Sundae and Sundi; about 45 years ago, on a Sunday afternoon, John M. Scott…and Chester Platt were having their usual Sunday confab.…Mr. Platt then came up to the soda fountain where I was holding forth, asking for two dishes of ice cream, and on each he placed a candied cherry, then, after considering a bit he poured cherry syrup over them.*

It's interesting to note that after the sundae's introduction, the ledger shows Christiance received a sizable raise, enough so that he bought the pharmacy and ran it through the 1920s. As is the case with so many local food stories, the location of the first ice cream sundae is up for debate. Wisconsin's Two Rivers has tried to debunk Ithaca's claim. They too have a reverend, a Sunday treat and a sundae result. Their claim escalated when a 2006 city council resolution issued by the Town of Two Rivers

Chester Platt, as photographed circa 1910, just years after he reportedly assisted with the creation of the first ice cream sundae. *Library of Congress.*

demanded that Ithaca "cease and desist" from its continued claims of being the "Birthplace of the Ice Cream Sundae." The resolution cited smiles on children's faces, burgeoning waistlines on adults' figures and the fact that Two River is the "coolest city" in America's dairy land as being grounds for such an action. I have to think the resolution has tongue firmly planted in cheek and spoon solidly set in a delicious canoe-shaped glass bowl filled with ice cream, whipped cream and chocolate sauce. Perhaps an eventual agreement to share the distinction will be the proverbial cherry on top.

Frozen Custard

It would be an insult to frozen custard fans across the region to pass over this rich, creamy addition to brain freeze. Frozen custard differs from ice cream in that it benefits from the addition of egg yolks, making it a richer finished product. Additionally, the machine that whips up the custard incorporates less air, so you get a dense result with a thick, unctuous texture and mouthfeel. It all starts with Upstate's pristine dairy—milk and cream—so both ice cream and frozen custard have a head start when they start Upstate. There are temples to this sweet treat, and they seem to be less of an ice cream shop and more of that old-time roadside stand. Next time you are in the region, do a taste test and see which you prefer. If you're like the majority of people asked, your answer will be *both*.

The beauty of a road trip through Upstate New York reveals farm-fresh milk in clear bottles with possibly a hint of cream that has risen to the top. You might sample award-winning eggnog or ice cream that blends just picked mint and perfectly ripened strawberries. You can enjoy a cheese plate with French-inspired soft cheeses and assertive Cheddars that will make you long for a barstool in a British tavern. Maybe breakfast is a perfectly tart goat's milk yogurt parfait and house-made bread slathered in golden butter. Now if that isn't a perfect food tour, I don't know what is. For "Where to Go" recommendations, refer to the section at the back of this book.

• • • • • • • • • •

Recipe: Homemade Yogurt

Ralph Waldo Emerson once said, "Adopt the pace of nature: her secret is patience." That applies to making homemade yogurt. It takes little expertise but a lot of patience. The reward is turning a ½ gallon of milk into a tubful of fresh, unctuous yogurt, saving you trips to the market and plenty of money. And it is so simple to make. Having a thermometer is key, and an Instant Pot makes this child's play.

Heat 2 quarts (½ gallon) of whole or low-fat milk in a pot over medium heat, stirring occasionally, until it reaches 180F/82C. Lower the heat to simmer and hold the milk at 180F/82C for 10 minutes, skimming the film that collects at the top.

Let the milk cool to 115F/43C; this takes between 30 and 45 minutes.

Stir 2 tablespoons of store-bought plain yogurt (whole or 2 percent is fine) into a small bowl and stir in a few tablespoons of the milk—this will temper the mixture and avoid curdling. Stir this back into the pot.

Cover the pot and place it in an oven that is turned off, but with the light on, for 6 to 12 hours. The ambient heat is enough to incubate the yogurt. The longer it sits, the more the texture will improve, and the flavor will be tangier.

You want your yogurt to stand up to the standing spoon test, thick and unctuous. *Author photo.*

Chill the yogurt for several hours before eating. For thicker, Greek-styled yogurt, strain the mixture through a coffee filter or cheesecloth that you place in a strainer over a large bowl for at least 4 hours. The longer it strains, the thicker it becomes. The whey that collects in your bowl can be used in a myriad of ways.

If you have a yogurt maker or Instant Pot, follow their directions for heating and incubating the milk and yogurt.

Chapter 7

DRINKING UP NEW YORK

Alcohol does not solve any problems, but then again, neither does milk.
—John Wayne

It seems fitting, based on John Wayne's comment, to follow up our chapter on dairy with a boozy topic. For that, we head to the Finger Lake region of Upstate New York. In his love letter and aptly named book *Wines of the Finger Lakes*, Peter Burford shared an ancient Iroquois legend that the Great Spirit was asked to point to the most beautiful place on earth. He was said to have set his hands on the ground just south of what would be Lake Ontario. As his fingers drew away, the imprints filled with water and formed the Finger Lakes. This imagery is beautiful. The more literal among us might point instead to the scientific explanation that receding glaciers carved out the eleven Finger Lakes nearly twelve thousand years ago. Whichever theory you choose to believe, the result is the same: a geographically majestic region that also happens to support and sustain the growth of wine grapes. While the winters in the Finger Lakes (FLX for short) are decidedly colder than in other wine-growing locales such as Bordeaux, the lake effect is optimal for grape development. In his 1907 report on *The Grapes of New York*, U.P. Hedrick, who was stationed at the New York Agricultural Experiment Station, wrote,

> *The climate is exceptionally favorable for the grape grower….It is, if anything, of more importance than the land….A grape climate as near*

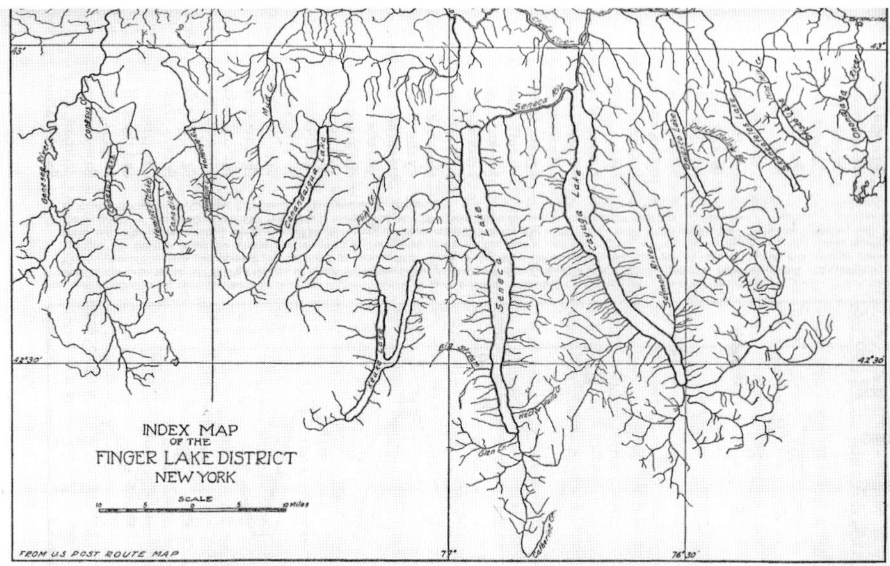

This 1914 map shows perfectly how the Finger Lakes region got its well-deserved name. *Binge, Edward A.; Juday, Chauncey (1914) Limnological study of the Finger Lakes of New York, Bulletin of the United States Bureau of Fisheries, vol. 32, 1912, Washington, DC: Government Printing Office.*

> *perfection as that of this region is indeed rare. The influence of the lake in modifying the temperature of the region is the chief climate factor.…It is common knowledge that large bodies of water temper cold winter weather, hold back vegetation in spring, equalize night and day temperatures of summer, lengthen the growing season and ward off autumn frosts.*

I Heard It Through the Grapevine

The soil, or terroir as the French would say, in this part of Upstate New York is rocky and sloped, filled with alkaline from shale, which supports the vines' need to struggle to survive. This confluence of optimal conditions makes the FLX a prime spot to produce some very distinguished wines. The area has a long history and love affair with nurturing the delicate fruit and coaxing the most cultivated flavors from it. Like all good love affairs, it begins slowly, builds to a fevered pitch and cools slightly, and then the fire is rekindled and burns even brighter. Such is the case with the Finger Lakes' history with wine. As early as the sixteenth century, Thomas Pinney noted in *A History of Wine in America*, explorer Giovanni Verrazzano commented favorably on the grapevines he observed in the area: "Many vines, growing naturally, which growing up, tooke [*sic*] hold of the trees as they doe [*sic*] in Lombardie.…Without all doubt they would yield excellent wines." The vines he observed were most likely the species native to Upstate New York called *Vitis labrusca*. Hedrick described those as being "foxy" and "musky" with notes of gunpowder. This species included Catawba, Isabella and the Concord grape, and because they are indigenous to the region, they were well suited to the climate. He could have also described the relationship between wine and the Finger Lakes as going together like a parishioner and his clergy, as the connection between wine and the church runs as deep as Seneca Lake.

Hedrick points to Deacon Elijah Fay, who in 1818 in the Chautauqua district, cultivated native grapes, those indigenous to the region. By 1830, Fay had eked out 10 gallons of passable wine. His attempts never went much further, and he remains a minor figure in New York's wine-growing history. In the Central Lakes District, specifically near Keuka, Canandaigua and Seneca, other men of the cloth were dabbling with grapevines as well. In 1829 Hammondsport, at the south end of Keuka

An 1893 drawing showing the full process of fermenting native grapes. *Library of Congress, C. Mitzky & Co.*

Lake, dubbed the Rhine of America, where the native grape vastly outnumbers the residents, divine intervention took hold. Reverend William P. Bostwick arrived in town to offer spiritual leadership. He also recognized the need for sacramental wine. He planted two native grapes, Isabella and Catawba, in his rectory garden. Bostwick's efforts were met by Andrew Reisinger, whose four or five hundred acres made a significant contribution to Keuka Lake's wine-growing reputation. According to Laura Winter Falk in her book *Culinary History of the Finger Lakes*, within thirty years there were three thousand acres of grapevines in this district. By 1900, that number had increased tenfold. Much of the development was owed to the sharing and grafting of vines by neighbors and villagers. Creating wine was apparently a commandment, as another man of the cloth (and the wine glass), Deacon Samuel Warren of Livingston County, rivaled Bostwick's grape-growing prowess. On his thirty-three-acre farm

This 1899 rendering depicts the many aspects of the Pleasant Valley Wine Company. *From the book* Outings on the Lackawanna: Summer Excursion Routes and Rates.

in York, he too planted Isabella and Catawba grapes for sacramental wine. According to Lifeinthefingerlakes.com, Warren's first vintage in 1832 produced 20 gallons, a good start but hardly enough for his parishioners to enjoy a robust holy communion. In a funny coincidence, he ran an ad for his wine in an evangelical publication, which printed it alongside an ad for hotels focused on temperance. By 1853, he had improved his yield to 3,400 gallons. His winery, however, failed to survive as the newly built railroad ran right through his property, and the business ceased to exist. That was not the fate for Catholic Bishop Bernard McQuaid, who established his winery in Livingston County. There, in 1872, he began producing sacramental wine, a venture that is still operational today.

You might wonder if residents of these towns were in a constant stupor. Happily, they shared their bounty when in the mid-1800s they began to ship their grapes to other areas. The first to do so was J.W. Prentiss, who had moderate success when in 1854 he shipped a ton of Isabella grapes to New York City. Using apple barrels, the product reached the market in fair condition and fetched a rousing fifteen cents per pound. The industry continued to thrive, and in 1860 the Pleasant Valley Wine Company was formed, making it the first of its kind in America. In 1961, having sustained considerable growth and surviving prohibition, Pleasant Valley was acquired by another one of the "big four." That company, Taylor Wines, was also based in Hammondsport and was formed in 1880 by William Taylor, a cooper by trade. Widmer's Wine Cellars, the third wine company of note, under the guidance of Swiss immigrant John Jacob Widmer, dared to locate outside of Hammondsport in Naples in 1888. A 1974 *New York Times* article called "Wine Talk" explores some of Widmer's biggest achievements, including their Lake Niagara white.

A Sparkling History

In a bubbly development, by the early 1900s, Keuka Lake had become the epicenter of wine and champagne production in the FLX. You might be surprised to know that before the 1936 act that restricted any sparkling white wine outside of the Appellation d'Origine Contrôlée (AOC) from calling itself Champagne, Upstate New York was a leader in its production. The International Wine and Food Society points to Charles Davenport Champlin, a native of France, who recognized that Keuka Lake had much in common with his beloved homeland. Champlin was a partner in the aforementioned Pleasant Valley Wine Company, where he endeavored to produce New York champagne. After several less-than-sparkling attempts, in 1870, he poached two French winemakers to come to Hammondsport and nurture his champagne. They succeeded at the 1873 Vienna Exposition,

This illustration shows the bon vivants of 1897 enjoying champagne at a resort on the shores of Keuka Lake. *Library of Congress, Delaware, Lackawanna and Western Railroad Company*

Frank was an innovator and driving force in new techniques and methods to grow the best wine grapes. *Wikimedia Commons, Fedorov Yevhenii.*

where Champlin debuted his "Great Western Champagne," taking home first prize. By the end of that century, there were more than fifty wineries, producing close to seven million bottles of New York champagne being sold annually, with 90 percent of all American sparkling wine coming from Steuben County.

Urbana Wines, the fourth major player, began in 1865 and produced its signature product, Golden Seal Champagne. They took the area's vine growing to a new level when in 1934 they brought in Charles Fournier. Fournier was quite a long way from his home of Reims, France, and his position as chief winemaker at the renowned Veuve Clicquot when he took the lead at Urbana. Burford calls him no less than a visionary, as he took Urbana's Gold Seal champagne across the country and entered it at the California State Fair, where it earned first place. It was Fournier who encouraged the region to plant not just native grape but *Vitis vinifera*, the premier species found in southern Europe and parts of Asia. While attending a seminar at the Geneva Experiment Station, Fournier met Dr. Konstantin Frank. Frank, a Ukrainian with a doctorate in viticulture and agronomy, brought his expertise to New York as he worked on berry research. It was Frank who championed the growth of vinifera grapes, varieties that were not native to the Finger Lakes and some felt would assuredly not survive the cold climate. *Vitis vinifera* are most at home in southern Europe and parts of Asia and are the grape we most readily associate with fine wine such as pinot noir and chardonnay. Frank developed a unique approach that yielded twelve vinifera varieties, grafting over 250,000 grapevines. Burford called him "a force of nature." Combining efforts, Frank and Fournier brought the FLX into modern-day wine production on a level that naysayers thought was unattainable.

CRISP AND DRY

Another central player in the Finger Lakes story was Hermann J. Wiemer. A German immigrant, Wiemer was approached by O-Neh-Dah vineyards, one of the leading producers of sacramental wine. After a decade of working for others, he ventured out on his own and founded his vineyard on Seneca Lake. A turning point in his career came during the Christmas Massacre. No, Rudolph was not euthanized, but rather a drastic temperature disparity from a balmy thirty degrees on Christmas Eve 1980 to twenty degrees below on Christmas Day devastated the vines, threatening those that Wiemer had advanced. However, on closer inspection, Wiemer discovered his vines were intact, able to survive what Evan Dawson deemed in his beautiful book *Summer in a Glass* "a nuclear meltdown." This Christmas miracle encouraged Wiemer to pursue his dream of growing vinifera grapes, which led to his great success in perfecting the area's premier Riesling, an off-dry white wine that mimicked the more well-known German product. This changed the wine landscape literally and figuratively for generations to come. Thera Clark, the sommelier at Wiemer, is energized by the wine forecast in New York; she emphatically told me that "FLX understands how to put dry Rieslings on the world stage."

The Central Lake District wasn't the only wine-producing region in Upstate New York. Hudson Valley boasted thirteen thousand acres of grapes in 1890, but due to poor conditions and management, that number soon dropped off. Not to be overlooked, Croton Point and New Paltz boasted some credible vineyards, and a French vintner, John Jacques, might be noted as having the oldest actual vineyard in New York, located in Washingtonville. Hedrick gives a substantial nod to Hudson Valley for not only cultivating grapes but

A who's who of notable winemakers and viticulturists in the Finger Lakes, *left to right*: Hermann J. Wiemer, Dr. Konstantin Frank, Walter Taylor (*standing*) and Helmut Becker. *Wikimedia Commons, DBlomgren.*

also promoting a profound interest in horticulture. The area nurtured more varieties and trained grape growers in how to finesse and cultivate with a defter hand. The final notable grape-growing region was Niagara, home of its eponymous grape, the Niagara. They soon learned that their forte was in table grapes, rather than wine, and little expansion ensued.

Temper That

In a moment of "timing is everything," the region's expertise in wine and champagne collided head-on with the growing temperance movement, which had serious ramifications. How ironic that Seneca Lake now became the hub of both wine production and efforts by women such as Elizabeth Cady Stanton and Susan B. Anthony to champion sobriety and women's rights. Upstate New York's wine legacy had now come full circle. The politically incorrect joke of a rabbi, a priest and a minister walking into a bar could easily have described the Finger Lakes during Prohibition, as sacramental wine was exempt from the Volstead Act. That gave way to a boom in kosher wine production in the Finger Lakes. This overly sweet syrupy liquid that we loosely call wine favors the Concord grape that is grown in Upstate New York. And while our perception of kosher wine has evolved, as it's less about the grape and more about the process that renders a wine kosher, Upstate New York became the temple of kosher wine production. Concord grapes traveled from Upstate to New York City, where Monarch Wine produced kosher wine under the label of Manischewitz. Today Manischewitz wine is produced in Canandaigua, New York, under rabbinical supervision. It continues to be the no. 1 kosher wine brand in America. Those same grapes became the basis for Concord grape juice, and Kedem, another kosher producer, founded by the Herzog family, became the chief player in that field. While not produced in Upstate New York, their grape juice made from Upstate Concord grapes has made them a household name and is the reason most parents need a good upholstery cleaner.

The Concord grape is abundant in Upstate and has the perfect sweetness for making ceremonial wine and grape juice. *Wikimedia Commons, J.T. Lovett Company*

The grapes of New York have a long and storied history from their native roots to their world-class achievements. The one thing they don't do is become raisins, which some say are grapes punished for their sweetness. For that, you need California grapes, which have more concentrated sugar and make for a better wrinkled snack. But FLX's wine story doesn't stop here, it's just the beginning. Those like Clark whose enthusiasm for wine is palpable describe the FLX wine industry as "honoring the history and realizing the moment in time that's special with promise toward the future." There are some exciting developments and accommodations to climate change that make wine growing in Upstate New York an intoxicating adventure. Not only has the wine industry boomed, receiving recognition even Dr. Frank could not have envisioned, but it also has led to a communal tide of cheesemongers, artisanal bakeries and world-class dining, elevating the Finger Lakes as not just another nice place to drive through but a place to stop and spend some time. To explore the area's best sips, look at the "Where to Go" section at the back of the book.

BEER WITH US

From south to north, New York State has a long history of brewing beer. No doubt Rheingold and Schaeffer put Brooklyn on the beer brewing map, but Upstate New York has a heady history as well. It's estimated by the Beer Institute that beer consumption by legal-aged drinkers is about 28.2 gallons per person per year. North Dakotans consumed twice that on average and New Yorkers slightly below. That statistic would come as news to the seventeenth-century settlers of New Netherland, who brought with them a tradition of brewing ale, cementing Upstate New York as a hub for the brewing industry. It would take volumes to review all the breweries and tastemakers who left their imprint, but here's an overview that you can use to impress your friends at your next round of beer pong.

A marriage brewed to help grow the Gansevoort empire. Pictured is a reproduction of a 1788 painting of Catherina Van Schaick, the future Mrs. Peter Gansevoort. *Wikimedia Commons, Ezra Ames from the Albany Institute of History and Art.*

The state's capital is a good place to begin, as it's where the industry got a strong start back in the seventeenth century. Welcome Harmen Gansevoort, who traveled from his home in Groningen, a northern region in the Netherlands, to what was then called Beverwijck, renamed Albany when the British controlled the colony in 1664. Harmen's family were beer brewers back in the Netherlands, so it was natural for him to take advantage of the hops-growing area and produce beer near his new home. We have genealogical records from the Schenectady digital library to thank for the family tree that outlined Gansevoort's rise. In a move driven perhaps by commerce as much as affection, he married the daughter of another brewer and established his family as the sudsy top of Albany society. His residence and brewery were located at the corner of Market Street and Maiden Lane, where it operated for 150 years. In a series of unions that makes six degrees of separation seem like child's play, the Gansevoorts intermarried with the Van Schaicks, another brewing legend in the area. Suffice it to say that these families secured Albany's prominence in the business of beer.

The Albany Institute featured an exhibit that celebrated the four-hundred-year-old industry that developed in the capital region. In the mid-seventeenth century, twelve breweries were operating in the area, which continued to thrive through the post–Revolutionary War period. Within one hundred years, Albany had become an epicenter of beer as the New York hops industry flourished. By the 1860s, there were more than thirty breweries, one notable being John Taylor & Sons, at the time the largest brewery in the country. Alone, they could produce a whopping-hopping 200,000 barrels a year, including their most popular beer, Albany XX Ale. Like so many other industries that initially benefited from the Erie Canal, Albany breweries experienced a decline in sales as competition from other states grew. With the innovation of shipping products by rail, the Erie Canal proved to be less of an advantage. Not only was there now greater competition, but the country was also filling their steins with German-style lager rather than ale, creating less of a demand for the Albany style of brew. Prohibition landed another blow as bootlegged alcohol could be produced in small quantities while commercial beer brewing required more large-scale efforts. It was harder to conceal a brewing facility than a backyard moonshine still. For all those reasons, beer producers suffered in the area and saw a great drop in production.

Traveling a bit south to the Hudson Valley, meet the Vassars of Vassar College fame. In 1861, the patriarch of the family endowed an elite women's college in his hometown of Poughkeepsie, and he made his fortune as a brewer. Like so many others of the time, Vassar's family immigrated to New York from England seeking religious freedom. Back home, according to Vassar's records, they were farmers and brickmakers and brewed ale to supplement their living. The story goes that one of Matthew Vassar's uncles brought English barley from Norfolk, and the family, who lived in Dutchess County, began making ale. Vassar moved to Poughkeepsie, where he built his empire. By 1837, his British-styled ale sold for close to six dollars a barrel, and he was producing upward of fifty thousand barrels a year. He secured his legacy not with his beer prowess but his civic activities and through Vassar College. As Larry Hertz wrote in the Vassar alumnae quarterly, Vassar College "was built on a foundation of malt, barley, hops and yeast." In a fun endeavor, students at the college recently set out to re-create Vassar's original ale. They noted it packed a punch and was lights out stronger over beer and ale enjoyed today.

Not to pale in comparison, Utica had a great tradition of brewing pale ale as well. Bob Allers, a former teacher and local authority on coopering and breweries, knows all there is to know about Utica's beer legacy. While Rome had about a dozen breweries, Utica had close to forty. Inman's Brewery, which started in 1801, was said to be the first. In the 1800s, Aller noted that Oneida County was considered the hops capital of the world. It was the job of the women and children to pick the hops from the bines (not vines) as they were light and could be easily handled. It was the Matt family who in the mid-1800s made Utica a real player in the industry. FX Matt established the West End Brewing Company in 1888, which continues to thrive today. They survived Prohibition by shifting production to soft drinks, and after the Eighteenth Amendment was repealed, they were the first in the country to obtain a license to sell beer, which they called Utica Club. Their premier label is Saranac, and their IPA is the winner of four gold medals.

There is a resurgence of breweries in Upstate New York, where craft beer, brewpubs, microbreweries and farm breweries are filling mugs from the Hudson Valley to Western New York. Spurred by an incentive known as the Farm Brewery License, small brewers who agreed to use 90 percent locally sourced ingredients by 2024 receive tax benefits and other financial rewards. While Suffolk County boasts the most breweries in New York State, according to a 2019 survey conducted by Syracuse.com, Monroe, Erie, Onondaga, Ontario, Ulster, Dutchess, Steuben and Orange all make the top ten. Craft beer is giving the big names a run for their money, and nowhere is that industry more popular than in Upstate New York. Feel like bar hopping? Check out the "Where to Go" section at the back for some suggestions.

It's Five O' Clock Somewhere

There's more to Upstate New York's imprint on alcohol than wine and beer. The region has some pretty interesting cocktail history and some other drinks to imbibe whose origins could make your head spin more than the drink itself. Let's start with the obvious, the cocktail. If we can be sure of nothing else related to the origin of the cocktail, we can agree on its definition. *Merriam-Webster* defines a cocktail as "usually an iced drink of wine or distilled liquor mixed with flavoring ingredients." One of the earliest mentions of cocktails in print appeared in *The Balance, and Columbian Repository*, a Hudson, New York newspaper that published miscellaneous information of the day. On page 146 in volume 5 in their communication section, which appears to be letters to the editor, you can find this entry. Please note that the convention of using an *f* for an *s* was adopted from Old English and quickly died out, as it is very confusing. I left the text as is as a nod to the original and to give your brain a workout.

> *As I make it a point, never to publish any thing (under my editorial head) but what I can explain, I shall not hefitate to gratify the curiofity of my inquisitive coorefpondent: -Cock tail, then is a stimulating liquor, compofed of Fpirits of any kind, sugar, water, and bitters—it is vulgarity called bittered fling, and is fuppofed to be an excellent potion, inasmuch as it renders the heart ftout and bold, at the fame time that it fuddles the head. It is faid alfo, to be of great ufe to a democratic candidate: becaufe, a perfon having fwallowed a glafs of it, is ready to fwallow any thing elfe. Edit. Bal.*

That doesn't mean the cocktail was invented in Hudson, but the fact that a local paper reported on it could mean the drink might have first appeared in the area. Dan Cazentre, in his book *Spirits & Cocktails of Upstate New York*, looks at several historical claims related to the cocktail, and he comes back with evidence that does point to the area. In a somewhat convoluted reference, author James Fenimore Cooper in his book *The Spy* tells of the cocktail having been served at a tavern in Westchester County—yes, I know that's downstate. However, Cooper was an Upstater who spent time in Lewiston, a small community that sits along the Niagara River. It was there that it was reported a barkeep placed a rooster's feather in a drink and it thereafter became known as a cock-tail. Quite possibly it was his exposure to that occurrence that informed Cooper's account.

Beef on weck, with the perfect bun with flecks of salt and caraway, perfectly rare beef, oozing with its own juices, cozied up with a pickle and horseradish on the side. *Flickr photo credit Nick Gray*.

A balanced plate of Buffalo wings, plenty of dipping sauce, celery to quell the heat and a beer to wash it all down. *iStock photo credit bhofack2*.

Above: Chicken riggies is rustic and familiar and reminds anyone eating it of an Italian Sunday supper. *iStock photo credit rudisill.*

Left: The garbage plate's name doesn't quite say it all, as the components are all delicious and together, uniquely compatible. *Author photo*.

With its vibrant grape color and flavor plus an interesting mouthfeel, this pie is very satisfying. *iStock photo credit bhofack2*.

Half mooners, harlequins or black and whites: no matter what you call them, they are delicious. *Author photo.*

Could this Tully burger have been the inspiration for the Big Mac? *iStock photo credit OlgaMiltsova.*

A fully loaded michigan, with onions on top, rather than buried beneath the dog. *iStock photo credit bhofack2*.

Nothing upside down about this pizza, where the crust has the right chew, the cheese is in every bite and the sauce is divine. *Author photo*.

Left: Notice how the pepperoni curls up like a cup, with the edges charred and the centers pooling with goodness. *iStock VeselovaElena*.

Below: Try a slice of tomato pie next time you want a savory bite that won't burn the roof of your mouth. *Author photo*.

Right: Salt potatoes, slightly crispy with a balanced salinity on the outside, creamy and fluffy on the inside. *iStock photo credit rudisill.*

Below: Spiedies, a taste of Abruzzi, seasoned and grilled to perfection. *Flickr photo credit David Berkowitz.*

This versatile condiment known as Thousand Island dressing was born in the Upstate and is loved across the globe. *iStock Photo Credit: Fermate.*

You might know them as Utica greens, but locals name them for the chef who prepares them. *Wikimedia Commons, Buffaboy.*

What could be more perfect than wine and cheese with an amazing vista of the Finger Lake region. *Long Shadows, stock.adobe.com.*

This 1840 oil on canvas shows the joy of traditional cider-making in Upstate New York. *William Sidney Mount, Metropolitan Museum of Art.*

Top left: Mozzarella sticks are delicious when dipped in marinara sauce, or go Upstate and try a sweet raspberry dunk. *Wikimedia Commons, Joseph Nicolia*.

Top right: Now that's how you do Cornell chicken. *Chantal Liam, Unsplash*.

Bottom: Catch your dinner in any of Upstate's freshwater rivers and streams. *Clay Banks, Unsplash*.

Head to Upstate's farmer's markets for fresh-picked produce such as garlic and peppers. *Sofia-lorinc, Unsplash.*

Anything topped with freshly made succotash is inviting and delicious. *Kelly Sue, Flickr.*

Left: Fish Fry Friday is an Upstate tradition with succulent haddock and a crispy crust. *Leonie Clough*.

Below: It's Christmas every day when you visit Saratoga and crack into a satisfyingly sweet peppermint pig. *Author photo*.

Right: Grab the car and the kids and head to Upstate New York for autumn apple picking. *Noah Zeitlin, Unsplash*.

Below: Pear picking in Montgomery County is a fun fall family activity. *Sebastian Enrique, Unsplash*.

Top: Mountain air, oversized swimming pools and endless chaise lounges represented the vibe felt throughout the Borscht Belt resorts. *Library of Congress, John Margolies Roadside America Photograph Archive*.

Middle: The only thing that could make a bowl of spaghetti even more perfect is too much cheese baked on top. *Courtesy of Chef's restaurant, Buffalo, Greg Merkley*.

Bottom: Since 1820, fairgoers have enjoyed burgers and pretty much anything and everything at the Erie County Fair. *Wikimedia Commons, Martybiniasz*.

Next time you think pancakes, think Upstate New York. *Unsplash, Leighann Blackwood.*

The cherry on the top of Upstate's sweet contributions could just be the invention of the ice cream sundae. *VD photography, Unsplash.*

It's worth exploring that female tavern owner and her legendary connection to the cocktail. In a "when fact meets fiction" story, Cooper's fictional character named Betty Flanagan might just have been based on the Lewiston real-life barkeep Catherine "Kitty" Hustler. There are extensive reports, especially circulating around Lewiston, that she did indeed put a cockerel feather in a drink. They are so invested in this version of the story that one can take a tour of the area with a woman dressed like Kitty. Part of her shtick is to tell the story of the cocktail using these words.

> *Tomas and Catherine Hustler opened a tavern in Lewiston....Upon occasions, the Hustlers were even known to entertain a young naval officer named James Fenimore Cooper....They supposedly began to serve drinks mixed from several liquors and stirred with a rooster's tail feather....A young French officer was said to have stood and toasted Mrs. Hustler saying, "Viva la cocktail!"*

If you visit Lewiston, you'll find a marker at Center and Eighth Streets where Hustler's Tavern stood. The sign there reads, "Birthplace of the

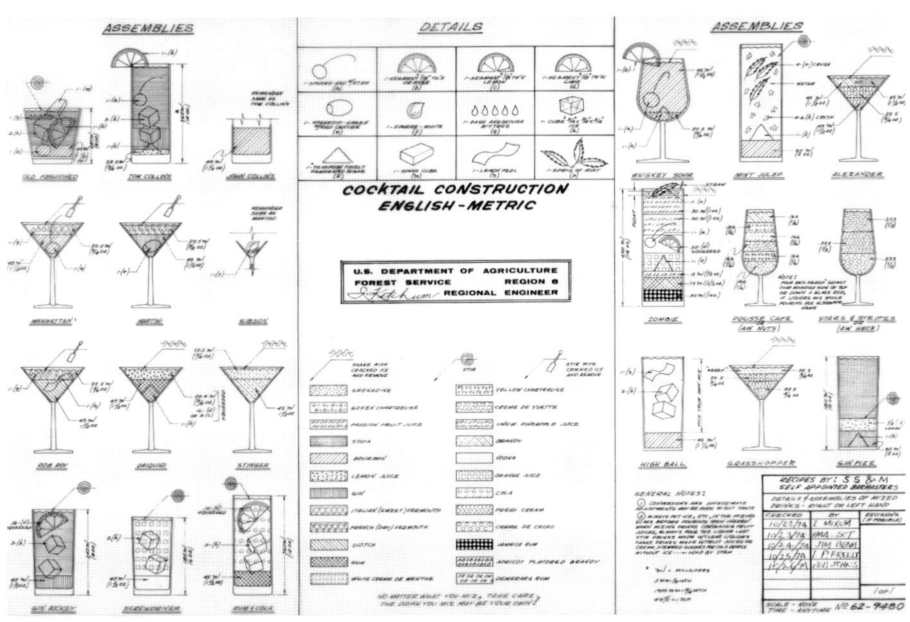

Illustrated guide to help construct the perfect cocktail. *Wikimedia Commons, National Archives Catalog Cleve "Red" Ketcham.*

A child of Upstate New York Jerry Thomas was the bartender's bartender, as illustrated in this 1862 drawing. *Wikimedia Commons, illustrated by Samuel Putnam Avery.*

cocktail." We cannot pinpoint the definite origin of the cocktail, but David Wondrich, whose book *Imbibe* is the drinking person's Bible, feels that cocktails originated within "the triangle between New York City, Albany, and Boston." For proud Upstaters, that's as close to a GPS confirmation of its origin as possible. Much as a maraschino cherry tops a gin tonic, the cherry on top of Upstate's connection to cocktails could just be Jerry Thomas. Known respectfully as "The Professor," Thomas was born in Sackets Harbor near the shores of Lake Ontario in northern New York. I am making no claim that he made his claim to fame in Upstate, but he was a child of the region and left an imprint quite large on the bartending scene through his book *The Bartender's Guide*. Two of Thomas's cocktails, the Saratoga Cocktail and the Saratoga Brace-Up, were a shoutout to a lifestyle comprising sipping a drink at the races, downing them at a fierce game of poker or just relaxing with a cocktail and enjoying a Saratoga sunset. Both appeared in his 1887 collection.

Thomas is joined by some colorful characters who lent their names to and imprints on Upstate's drinking traditions. Patsy McDonough comes to mind as a barkeeper in Rochester, New York. There at Lieders' Hotel, Brunswick McDonough wrote his *Bar-Keeper's Guide and Gentlemen's Sideboard Companion*. The title page describes the book as "a comprehensive and practical guide for preparing all kinds of plain and fancy mixed drinks and popular beverages of the day," written by someone who has had "25 years' experience in many of the leading bars in this country." The book is filled with cocktail and mixed drink recipes and features lots of ads for local roadhouses, breweries and even a doctor who specialized in "nervous diseases," perhaps for those who imbibed too much. One of the concoctions McDonough included was called the Stone Fence, which became a very popular Upstate drink. In a region that spawns a lot of apples, it makes sense that drinks would feature hard cider. The Stone Fence, McDonough's entry no. 218, adds bourbon whiskey to the hard cider to create a drink that packs a punch. Speaking of punch, McDonough's book shares over a dozen punch recipes with exotic ingredients like arrack and Jamaican rum.

Punch Bowl

Punch became a real craze, especially in the Albany region. Punch, whose name derives from the Hindi word *panch*, which means "five," refers to the five ingredients that happily swim together in the bowl: rum, water, sugar, juice and spice. The Albany Institute of History & Art built an entire exhibit around the punch bowl when they featured recipes served by some of Albany's most elite residents. The Van Rensselaers favored Lime Rum Shrub, which is similar to today's gimlet, while Mrs. Harmon Pumpelly Read was known to serve one that packed a punch, with way more than the requisite five ingredients, adding peach brandy, green tea and champagne to the mix. Should you get testy, you might want to down

Elaborately ornate Tiffany punch bowl circa 1873. *The Art Institute of Chicago.*

a Regents Punch designed by the New York State Board of Regents chancellor John Van Schaick Pruyn, who would have posed the multiple-choice question: Which ingredient would you not expect in punch? The correct answer would be raisins, which he put in his recipe along with seltzer and Madeira. It was said that in 1924 he served his punch in a bowl that once belonged to Daniel D. Tompkins, who served as New York state governor and vice president of the United States under James Monroe.

Imagine sliding into a booth and enjoying a century-old yuletide tradition at the Crystal Tavern. *Courtesy of the Crystal Tavern, Watertown, New York.*

Pruyn didn't have to go to the Caribbean to get rum for his punch. Cazentre noted that in 1750, Albany was home to seventeen rum distilleries. It was during excavation for a parking garage in 2000 that two rum distilleries were unearthed in Albany. Remnants of fermentation vessels were uncovered, giving credibility to Albany being a rum distilling hub. The rum was prepared in a more British, less Dutch-influenced fashion, and the distillery became known as Douw-Quackenbush Still House. In 1790, a local paper reported it could distill up to 220 gallons a day.

Rum was an essential ingredient in the Tom and Jerry, an Upstate New York drink that dates back over one hundred years. No cat and mouse mystery here: the drink was created in the 1820s by Englishman Pierce Egan to promote his book. It is a frothy, eggnog-like drink that is served hot in a brimming punch bowl. While its popularity has dwindled in most places, except perhaps some old-school bars in the Midwest, Upstaters have elevated this Christmastime favorite to an art form. No one in the area honors this drink more than the Crystal Restaurant in Watertown, where the Dephtereos family has been serving the yuletide specialty since 1928. This throwback establishment is home to one of the very last stand-up bars in the country and is a shrine to the Tom and Jerry. Revelers come mug in hand to scoop out their portion of this potion that heralds in the holiday season.

Just as you wouldn't leave your cocktail unfinished, we definitely shouldn't leave the topic and its relationship with Upstate unfinished. Enter Mamie Taylor, another colorful and flamboyant character in the tale of the cocktail. Mamie was a celebrated operatic singer and actor who, as reported in the *Post Standard*, a Syracuse newspaper, "was the prima donna...playing at Ontario Beach, near Rochester in 1899." When asked what she would want to drink after a long hot day, she favored a "long but not strong drink." The bartender created one with sparkling champagne, adding a bit of lemon, and the combination was an instant hit. It was aptly named the Mamie Taylor. The drink, according to australianbartender.com.au, became increasingly popular throughout the states and remained so until Prohibition. In a truly comical report, the *Salt Lake Herald* in 1902 printed a hilarious account related to the Mamie Taylor between a bartender at a posh hotel and an important guest. The story begins simply enough with the guest asking the bellboy to have the bartender prepare her a Mamie Taylor. The bartender, not being familiar with the drink, consulted a mixology guide, to no avail. He then was quoted as asking the bellboy "what kind of lady was she as to build, and he told me she looked as if she had never missed a meal...so I says [*sic*] to myself she's a good, strong, healthy woman and wants something to put some ginger in her system." The bartender took a jigger and blended scotch, old bourbon, a bit of port wine and sugar and topped it with nutmeg. Upon tasting the drink, the woman claimed, "That's not a Mamie Taylor, that was a Margie Williams." On his second attempt, he used curaçao, vermouth, Old Tom gin, a dash of orange bitters and a squirt of Jamaica rum. Despite finishing that drink as well, she exclaimed, "That wasn't a Mamie Taylor, it was a Jessie Bartlett." His next attempt she called an "over the Hills to the Poor House." On his last attempt, he said, "I put in enough whiskey to make her glad until July fourth." After finishing it, she quickly took a long nap, leaving him wondering if he got the drink right. For those who do want to know what went into a proper Mamie Taylor, Bill Sterritt, the bartender who perfected it in Upstate, used scotch whiskey and lime juice and topped it off with ginger ale; some consider it the forerunner to the popular Moscow Mule.

•••••••••

Recipe: Poached Pears in Riesling

As a nod to the delicious Riesling being produced in the Finger Lakes, and the bounty of fresh pears in the fall, enjoy this recipe where the two meld perfectly to create an impressively easy dessert.

About 4 to 6 servings
Start to finish: Under 30 minutes

1 ½ cups Finger Lakes Riesling
1 cup water
2 cinnamon sticks
6 Bartlett pears, peeled, cored and halved lengthwise
1 tablespoon vanilla extract
½ cup white raisins

Bring the wine, water and cinnamon sticks to a boil; reduce to a simmer; and add the prepared pears and vanilla. Cover and cook, over low heat, for about 20 minutes or until the pears are fork tender. Remove the pears to a bowl and raise the heat to medium-high. Cook until the liquid is reduced by half, about 10 minutes. Remove the cinnamon sticks and add ½ cup raisins (optional); cook for an additional 3 minutes. Cool the pears and sauce separately. When fully chilled, serve the pears with the sauce drizzled on top.

Chapter 8

HEALTH, HISTORY AND HORSES

Water, Water Everywhere

The natural wonders of Saratoga County in eastern New York State are a confluence of geographic markers. The county borders both the Hudson and Mohawk Rivers and is framed by the lowlands of the Hudson Valley to its south and east and the Adirondack Mountains to the northwest. With all these gifts from Mother Nature, perhaps none has defined the county more than the mineral springs that are the foundation of Saratoga's glory days. The first explorers came at the behest of Native Americans who in 1771 brought Sir William Johnson to see their "medicine spring." The name Saratoga derives from the Iroquois word Serachtague, which means "a place of swift water." The Indigenous Native Americans viewed the bubbling waters as the breath of their spirit god Manitou. In 1783, none other than George Washington was said to have been so enamored of the spring water that he tried to purchase a parcel of land near High Rock. Could his victory at the Battle of Saratoga be credited to the enriched waters that emboldened the soldiers? Probably not, but it makes for a good tale.

At the time of Saratoga's founding, you would have needed one hundred pairs of hands to provide enough thumbs to plug their cold-water geysers. The land sits on a fault, and the plates below create a natural layer that traps and enriches the water, keeping it at fifty-five degrees Fahrenheit, making them cold rather than hot springs. It also makes them eminently drinkable,

Visitors marveling at Saratoga Springs circa 1870. *NYPL Digital Collections.*

each with a differing taste, from salty to crisp and clean. And while they might smell of sulfur, there is no telltale flavor. The natural carbonation from the trapped carbon dioxide made it not only attractive as a digestif, but the water was said to be recuperative and therapeutic as well. This premise led to the town being known as "Queen of the Spas," and many health-conscious elite flocked there to bathe in the curative water and be hydrated by the springs.

A turning point for the city came in 1789, when Gideon Putnam, whom Saratogasprings.com and many others call Saratoga's founding father, began developing the area. He intended to create a spa-style resort in what appeared to be the wilderness. Arriving at Saratoga, he described it as a "forest with a few log houses and a mineral spring." In 1802, he built the Putnam Tavern, a boardinghouse that later became the Grand Union Hotel, whose illustrious guests included literary luminaries such as James Fenimore Cooper, Edgar Allan Poe and Nathaniel Hawthorne. Industrious entrepreneurs joined in turning Saratoga into what many called the "Las Vegas of the East." There was gambling at John Morrisey's Club House (later known as Canfield Casino) and Thoroughbred racing at what is the oldest racetrack in the country. As cited in *A Guide to the Empire State*, published by the Writer's Program in 1940, a passage from an 1841 guidebook described Saratoga as a mingling of "gentlemen of the turf, connoisseurs of the odd trick and amateurs of poker." For a time, the Grand was the largest hotel in the United States. It was Putnam's vision that laid out the development of Saratoga Springs. As demand increased and conservation measures were nonexistent, Saratoga's naturally carbonated springs became depleted. The main culprits were unregulated gas companies who abused the springs to extract carbonic gas for soft drinks. In 1911, the New York State Reservation was created, and happily, the springs were saved. However, now, only twenty-one springs remain in the entire town.

Visitors to Saratoga can sample the various "flavors" that each unique spring provides; some industrious ones bring bottles to fill and sample. Since 1872, Saratoga Spring Water has been bottling this naturally carbonated, mineral-rich H_2O. The water was termed "Saratoga Vichy" as an homage to the naturally carbonated French mineral springs. Jessie Morrison, in an article for Ediblemanhattan.com, noted that in 1903 the French Republic filed suit to prevent this labeling but lost the contest.

Just as Pitman described, this shows what was left of the original church in Saratoga Springs, a humble cabin in the woods. *Library of Congress.*

The expansive dining room at the Grand Hotel, circa 1900. *Library of Congress.*

The carbonated mineral water was pumped into a distinctive blue-green bottle that proudly sported a large *V*. Adam Madkour Jr., president and chief operating officer of Saratoga Spring Water, maintains tradition, as the water is bottled in the same plant it was back in 1872. However, some changes have invariably taken place. As you would guess, horse-drawn carriages are no longer the main means of transporting the water, which harkens back to the days when mineral water was considered medicinal and was delivered to nearby homes much as the milkman delivered dairy in the 1950s. The aquamarine bottles are now decidedly blue, to reflect the change from this being a medicinal water to a refreshing beverage. Most notably, the water now comes from a different source, a nearby spring that has a less minerally taste and is no longer naturally carbonated.

Saratoga Springs continues to attract people to see and sample the various spring waters, experience a Thoroughbred race and browse the remaining buildings that heralded the glitz and glamour of a bygone era. Their motto of "health, history and horses" remains as true today as it did when the town was first incorporated. No, you won't spot Diamond Jim Brady or his ilk roaming downtown, but do come with an empty water bottle and taste a bit of history.

Sip, Snack, Repeat

Perhaps no snack identifies with a city more than the potato chip does with Saratoga. It is almost indisputable that this ever-popular crunchie-munchie delight is the most popular savory snack out there and originated in Saratoga. Perhaps the legend of the potato chip is one of the best examples of food lore, as stories abound as to who created the first thinly sliced fried potato. There is a clear reference to "potatoes fried in slices or shavings" in an 1817 cookbook titled *The Cook's Oracle*, written by British physician William Kitchiner. It could certainly be the first written mention of the process, but many suspect the chip predated even that reference.

An African American/Native American cook named George Speck has widely been credited with developing the first potato chip to be served in a restaurant. Speck, who worked at Saratoga's Moon's Lake House, was known by the name George Crum, as that's what shipping and railroad magnate Cornelius Vanderbilt called him. In what could be seen as a racist slight, Vanderbilt renamed Speck to Crum, and the name stuck. The story goes that in 1853, Vanderbilt was not pleased with the fried potatoes he was served and asked Crum to make him a new batch. Either out of anger or a spark of creativity, Crum thinly sliced the otherwise fat slices, tossed them in a pan of hot oil and, voilà, created a potato chip. He served them to Vanderbilt, and to his great delight, they were a hit. So much so that in a restaurant Crum opened in Malta, New York, in 1860 called Crumbs House, he placed a basket of potato chips on every diner's table. But here's the problem with this story. Crum enjoyed a fair amount of acclaim as a

Guests enjoying the surroundings and freshly made potato chips at Moon's Lake House. *NYPL Digital Collections.*

chef in his own right, but you would be hard-pressed to find a mention of the potato chip in his lifetime. According to Greg Daugherty, who did considerable research on the topic for History.com, even though Crum might have been considered the first true celebrity chef, his 1914 obituary never listed the potato chip as one of his achievements. To complicate matters, in a case of sibling rivalry, his sister, Catherine Adkins Wicks, who died at the age of 103, claimed she was the true originator of the potato chip. She was warmly known as Aunt Kate and worked alongside Crum at Moon's Lake House. She told others that it was she, not her brother, who cut the potatoes paper-thin and accidentally dropped them in a pot of fat. When she discovered just how good they were, she had her aha moment. But wait, there's another claim to the title of potato chip inventor. That goes to another chef at Moon's Lake named Hiram S. Thomas. Daugherty reported that Thomas was once referred to as "the next Booker T. Washington," and it was he who invented the chip. His claim has less credibility, as he was the chef some forty years after chips were commercially available. Daugherty reported that Saratoga chips became the snack of the elite, as diners at upscale hotels and those aboard luxury liners were treated to potato chips alongside their fancy entrées. It became such a status symbol that even Tiffany sold a sterling silver Saratoga chip server to present the treat in style. What we can say with confidence is that Moon's Lake House in Saratoga was the birthplace of the American potato chip, and aren't we eternally grateful for that?

• • • • • • • • •

Recipe: Saratoga Vinegar and Salt Chips

These chips are great on their own or as a terrific accompaniment to a perfectly balanced club sandwich.

The trick to crisp chips is to slice them paper thin and soak them in cold water before frying. The water draws out the starch and allows them to crisp up more. Be sure to season them right after frying. You can certainly buy chips in a bag, but why would you want to after seeing how easy it is to make your own?

Makes about 4 cups of chips

2 Russet potatoes, about 1–1 ½ pounds, cleaned and scrubbed
2 cups vinegar, white, malt or apple cider or a combination
Vegetable oil
Olive oil
Sea salt
Vinegar powder, optional (found in specialty markets and available online)

Using a mandolin, slice the potatoes into very thin slices and drop into a large bowl of ice water. Let the potatoes soak for at least 30 minutes and up to 2 hours. Rinse the potatoes and clean out the bowl, removing any starchy residue that collected on the bottom. Place the potatoes back in the bowl and cover with vinegar for 30 minutes and up to 2 hours. The longer they soak, the more vinegary they will taste when cooked.

Fill a large Dutch oven with 2 parts vegetable oil (great smoke point and neutral flavor) and 1 part olive oil (for flavor) until it reaches about 3 inches. Use a thermometer to heat the oil to 360 degrees. While the oil heats, line a pan with paper towels and thoroughly dry the potatoes using a dishtowel.

Drop the potato slices into the oil in small batches; you don't want to overcrowd the pot. Cook for about 2 minutes, moving them in the oil using a slotted spoon or spider (one of my favorite all-around tools). Remove from the oil and place on the paper towel–lined tray. Drop the next batch.

Season the first batch with sea salt and additional vinegar powder if using. Place in a bowl and repeat until all the chips have been fried. Eat immediately, or they can stand for about an hour, but I doubt they'll last that long.

DO YOU WANT CHIPS WITH THAT?

Picture the perfect lunch. A crispy mound of potato chips sits in a tidy basket next to an appetizing sandwich. What sandwich do you see completing the picture? I would say nine out of ten lunch-goers would imagine a double-decker club sandwich. Those two go together like horse racing and Saratoga. Well, that's very convenient, as many maintain that the club sandwich was the creation of an ingenious chef from that town. As with many food origin stories, the club sandwich does not have one definitive version. Some foods are named for an acronym, such as the delectable MLT (mutton, lettuce and tomato sandwich) that Miracle Max of *Princess Bride* fame says is the only thing greater than true love. The name for the club sandwich might have a similar origin story, as some feel it derives from an acronym of the original ingredients of **C**hicken, **L**ettuce **U**nder **B**acon. Others suggest that it represents the backdrop where this sandwich was popularized, that being a clubhouse or clubby dining room where ladies who lunch were turned away and only gentlemen of a certain caliber were allowed entrance. The sandwich became the choice lunch of high rollers who enjoyed a mile-high sandwich with mounds of chicken, soft lettuce and crisp bacon. Ironically and unbeknownst to these elite diners, it could easily be that this sandwich was born out of convenience and frugality. It's posited that savvy kitchen staff or hungry late-night scroungers might have easily tossed the ingredients together after discovering leftover chicken, bacon and lettuce. They were piled onto toasted bread and served often as a double-decker delight. Claims from New York restaurateurs cite a sandwich built at the Union Club that predates the Saratoga sandwich. There, it is said that toasted graham bread was used as a conveyance for meat. Not sure that claim holds up, as there's no mention of the lettuce or bacon, so if I were a gambling girl, I'd stick with the Saratoga version.

The club sandwich found its way into mainstream America, with a recipe for its preparation featured in Good Housekeeping's *Everyday Cook Book* published in 1903. The recipe (and I use the term loosely) quite simply advised the preparer:

> Toast a slice of bread evenly and lightly butter it. On one half put, first a thin slice of bacon which has been broiled till dry and tender, next a slice of the white meat of either turkey or chicken. Over one half of this place a circle cut from a ripe tomato and over the other half a tender leaf of lettuce. Cover these with a generous layer of mayonnaise, and complete this delicious "whole meal" sandwich with the remaining piece of toast.

Just a typical day for the rich and famous at Saratoga's clubhouse. *Library of Congress.*

So ubiquitous was the sandwich that at the 1904 World's Fair held in St. Louis, even the Japan exhibit had a version of the sandwich. What once began as a double-decker sandwich, thought to have been so named as an homage to the double-decker club cars of early train travel, has now morphed into humongous sandwiches three layers high with the addition of onion jams and avocados, all forms of meats and toppings that would make mayonnaise angry.

Chapter 9

LET'S GO TO THE MOUNTAINS

THE BORSCHT BELT

In regional terminology, areas that share similar climates or product output are referred to as belts. There's the Snow Belt, where winter accumulations are the greatest, and the Corn Belt, where, you might guess, corn is in abundant supply. But there's an anomaly in this broad categorization that defines the Upstate enigma once known as the Borscht Belt. Certainly the area didn't brew batches of Russian or Ukrainian beet soup. The terrain wasn't awash in purplish and deep red colors. But it did define a cultural personality, one that was particularly inclusive of Eastern European Jewish Americans at a time when the country was not.

For nearly half a century, from the 1920s through the late 1970s, the Borscht Belt was the place to go for Jewish families to enjoy a winter getaway, take a break from the sweltering summer city heat or enjoy a show and copious amounts of kosher food. Located in the Catskill Mountains and sometimes referred to as the Jewish Alps, the Borscht Belt was a home away from home for 150,000 Jewish families each season. It was a bit Las Vegas mixed in with a shtetl feel. The Catskills sits in parts of Sullivan, Ulster and Orange Counties, making it an easy drive from New York City and its surrounding burbs. There were many reasons this area became a haven for Jewish guests. In a lovely piece for hospitalitynet.org, Stanley Turkey, a hotel consultant, enumerated one of the driving forces behind the pilgrimage to the area. He wrote, "The message came back to New York's lower East Side: the air was clean and fresh, the scenery beautiful, and the climate in July and August was cooler than the city." At the height of its popularity, there were

Lithograph print showing a view of the Hudson River and Catskill Mountains. *NYPL Digital Collections.*

nearly five hundred resorts and bungalow colonies that dotted the landscape and catered (literally and figuratively) to Jewish travelers from every social stratum. During this explosion of visitors, the impetus was different than it was after the Civil War when people came to the region to take in the bucolic atmosphere. It was a well-known secret that many hotels restricted two groups of people: "Hebrews and consumptives." This drove Jewish travelers to enclaves that were welcoming. The Catskills emerged as such a place, where Friday night services and kosher meals were commonplace. The big decision was a massive hotel or a bungalow colony. Generally, finances helped drive that decision, but the rallying cry was the same: "Let's go to the mountains."

THE SHOW GOES ON

If you've seen the movie *Dirty Dancing*, then you've had a glimpse into the Catskill resorts. There were activities daily, like summer camp for grownups, who could afford a summer of indulgence. You came for two things: the evening shows and the food. The shows featured headliners and up-and-comers who reached stardom through the Catskills. While singers and musicians like Barbra Streisand and Count Basie were headliners, it was the comedians who gave the lavish nightclubs their zing. From Shecky Greene to Milton Berle, Jerry Lewis to Joan Rivers, the hotels in the Catskills featured them all. You didn't need to be Jewish; you just needed that singular self-deprecating or observational humor that Jewish people could relate to. Whether you were at the two big hotels, the Concord and Grossinger's, or the other players like the Pines, Nevele, Kutschers or Browns, you were treated to these nightly shows.

The real show that defined the Catskill experience came three times a day in the massive dining rooms. My family were frequent winter visitors to the Concord Hotel, an institution on Kiamesha Lake. I can still remember the massive menu with absolutely no prices listed. You could order anything and everything and not pay a dime extra. Breakfast was pretty straightforward and the size of a lumberjack's dream. If you wanted waffles, pancakes and eggs for breakfast, no one would look at you funny. However, if you asked for a side of bacon, you would be quickly ushered out, as the hotel was strictly kosher.

A typical bungalow in the Catskills. *Library of Congress, John Margolies Roadside America Photograph Archive.*

The waiters became part of the nightly show. *Norman Levin.*

Kosher rules dictate you do not mix milk and meat, so the first two meals of the day were strictly dairy, with copious amounts of meat served at dinner. Typical lunch offerings were soup; yes, borscht both hot and cold was on the menu, as was schav, a green version made from bitter sorrel leaves. Lunch was the time to dabble in fish, be it baked, broiled or fried, and classic cold plates like mock chicken liver—yes, that was a thing. It was a plant-based chicken liver substitute—how millennial! There would be gefilte fish and marinated carp and blintzes with every topping imaginable. In a bit of unintended humor, the dietic option on one Grossinger's lunch menu included chocolate and vanilla ice cream and assorted luncheon cookies.

Dinner started out simply and built to an excessive crescendo. The appetizers were often chilled fruit cups or ripe melon, followed by trays of radishes, olives, carrot sticks and pickles. You would move on to soup, a consommé or delicate vegetable broth, and then, just for fun, they'd throw in a foreign dish such as chile con carne or chop suey. A typical exchange when ordering your main course might have been:

Diner: I'll have the brisket, the spring chicken and can that come with an order of prime rib?
Server: Of course, and would you want that with a side of stuffed cabbage?

The entrées sounded very French, and the descriptions I do believe were simply impressive words strung together with no real culinary meaning. Such a case would be the Boiled Yearling Fowl en pot, Bourgeoise. Dessert was light but plentiful as trays of sweets you never ordered found their way to your table. It might include Viennese pastries or more fresh fruit. There were even offerings that were low salt and low fat, as if those were ever ordered. While the resorts tried to take advantage of food from local farms and vendors, their massive kitchens featured a bit of everything, and as they needed to be kosher, many products were sent in from downstate.

You were assigned a table on your day of arrival, and that same server would be with you for your entire stay. The dining room was so massive that Alan Levy, in his 1974 article for the *New York Times*, reported that waiters were known to say to guests, "I'm sorry, sir, but your table isn't in my state." By day two you developed a rhythm, and your waiter knew your preferences and you his strengths. Could he score that extra plate of smoked salmon or bowl of pickled herring before the next table received theirs? If he did, he would be rewarded with a handsome gratuity at the end of your stay. I remember one year, we were less than impressed with our waiter and the tip reflected that. The waiter briskly followed us out of the dining room on our last morning, yelling, "What did I do wrong?!"

The dining room was massive as waiters and diners navigated their way to their reserved table. *Library of Congress, John Margolies Roadside America Photograph Archive.*

THE FRUGAL ALTERNATIVE

The bungalow colonies attracted a slightly different crowd; usually, guests stayed the entire summer and were on a tighter budget. These colonies sprang up across the area and were home away from home for many Jewish families and notably Holocaust survivors. They were built on the premise of community, as families returned season after season playing out the same rituals of swim, play cards, eat, play mahjong, kibbitz, play bingo, eat, repeat. Families often prepared their own meals; some ate communally or dared to dine out, which was a luxury. Vendors hawking their wares were regular visitors, selling products and familiar food. Phil Ratzer, in a 1958 piece titled "Once Upon a Time in the Catskills—A Memoir of Summer," wrote of "Ruby the Knish Man. He would drive his station wagon to the colony yelling 'Hey Knishes! Get your hot knishes! Buy a bagful and help send my wife to Florida!'" Arthur Tanney, in his writings on bungalow life, also recalled "the Knish man from Mountaindale" a.k.a. Ruby the Knish man. "He would arrive at our colony each and every Thursday afternoon, his truck laden with freshly roasted chickens, brisket, soup, kishka, cholent, and, of course, those marvelous knishes—potato and kasha." Ruby announced, in what Tanney called a gravelly Yiddish-inflected voice: "Ladies and gentlemen, this is Ruby the Knish Man. I'm now on the premises with my homogenized, pasteurized and recently circumcised potato knishes. Please folks come. I need the money." Perhaps Ruby was auditioning for a spot at the Concord Hotel nightclub, which, by the way, was the largest in the world. Tanney quipped that a mother's mahjong winnings could purchase a complete Shabbat dinner. Not to be overshadowed, there was also "Shimmy the Pickle King." Tanney recalled that his garlic sour pickles were "a thing of beauty."

If you do believe that all good things need to come to an end, then you'd be right about the heyday of the Borscht Belt. As cultural norms changed and Jews either assimilated to a greater extent or became more welcome in mainstream venues, the need for these safe havens was reduced. The hotels became the playground for people of different backgrounds, and the nightclubs, once the starting point for many new acts, became a swan song for others. People were not eating and drinking as they had been, and the excesses initiated by the post-Depression, postwar mentality gave way to the Atkins diet and health food craze. Dining rooms the size of football fields were passé, as those who could enjoyed more intimate surroundings and pared down minimalistic experiences. But we do love our comebacks, and the Catskills is no exception.

Playing canasta and mahjong was a favorite activity for the women in bungalow colonies. *Harvey Abrams Photography.*

The Catskills are ready for their second act. Steven Silverman, the author of *The Catskills*, feels "it is ripe for a revival." Small luxury hotel brands are bringing their style to the area with spas and fine dining that feed off the artisanal offerings in the region. One developer representing the posh Auberge Resorts explained, "Beyond the stunning landscape that makes for a picturesque backdrop, it was Hudson Valley's rich history, deep-rooted culture in the arts, culinary influence, and close-knit community that drew us in." The new incarnations are farmhouse-inspired with laid-back elegance. They convene with nature more than the need for glitzy entertainment and rely on the area's bounty. As an homage to this almost forgotten era, a group of Manhattanites cum Catskill dwellers began a project to pay tribute to the Borscht Belt. It is lovingly called the Catskills Borscht Belt Museum. The museum features memorabilia from the famed hotels, massive dining halls and camp-like activities. Recently, the New York State's Empire State Development (ESD) program awarded the museum a $650,000 grant to create the museum in Ellenville, in the former building that housed the Home National Bank.

As testimony to this reincarnation, Curbed New York reports that over the past few years, Sullivan County has seen a 25 percent increase in hotel rooms, with revenue coming close to matching that pace. That's not to say that some who favor the nightlife of casino gambling and glitzy entertainment cannot find all that currently in the Catskills. Resorts World Catskills, a 1.6-million-square-foot resort, is the reinvention of the Concord Hotel, taking over their former space and filling it with over 150 game tables and more than 2,000 slot machines. What has changed most is its target guests and the dining it offers. No longer trying to lure Jewish visitors, reports the *Daily News*, they have their eye on the Asian market. Their opening was adjusted to coincide with the Lunar New Year and their address is a number that is considered lucky in Chinese numerology. Perhaps the most stunning change is the food presented. Gone are the days when you could have triple entrées and twice as many desserts. Now you order from an Italian-inspired dinner menu courtesy of celebrity chef Scott Conant. His appetizers include a tower of shellfish, polenta with bacon and a rigatoni bathed in a pork ragu. Definitely not your kosher fare that reigned when the Concord was the king of kosher resorts. There's a focus on Chinese and Asian cuisine and a nod to the local scene with wings and burgers. Entertainment is no longer reserved for the Jewish comedian, as local bands representing the Hudson Valley such as Guilty as Hell and DJs such as Kev Watson keep the fun going. A return to the glory days is on the horizon. If you're looking to get your retro vibe on, visit the "Where to Go" section at the back of the book for suggestions.

• • • • • • • • •

Recipe: Bloom and Rose Knish

Courtesy of Zach Rosenbloom, restaurateur and owner of Bloom and Rose, Buffalo, New York

Our goal is to bring a unique perspective to the classic Jewish deli. We began our journey with knish, arguably the least known of any essential Jewish deli and likely the least respected. Our quest took us to Buffalo's blossoming farmers' markets, where we began sourcing many of our ingredients and seeking inspiration to funkify our flavors. We have to date offered well over 20 flavors, much of which we keep hyper seasonal with some going as wild as local mushroom and roasted peach. The recipe we have shared pays homage to the knish carts of old. Few things beat the classics, so we keep it simple with only a little bit of flair.

Knish Dough

1 ½ pounds all-purpose flour
2 teaspoons salt
2 tablespoons sugar

1 teaspoon baking powder
3 large eggs, whole (whisked)
⅔ cup canola oil
1 cup water
1 teaspoon distilled vinegar (prevents oxidation)

Traditional Potato Knish Filling

2 pounds potatoes (Yukon gold works best)
½ pound (2 sticks) unsalted butter (salted is fine)
2–3 yellow onions, diced (depending on size)
Salt and pepper to taste

To Make the Dough

1. Combine your dry ingredients together in a mixing bowl.

2. Mix your wet ingredients into your dry ingredients one by one. Start with your beaten eggs, followed by your oil, and finally the water and vinegar. Continue mixing until all ingredients are incorporated and the dough has a nice smooth texture. This will only take a few minutes in a mixer; it may take a bit longer if mixing by hand. The dough should be soft and easy to manipulate but not sticking to your hands; if your dough is a bit sticky, add a bit more flour. If your dough is stiff and seems dry, add a bit more water.

3. Once your dough is mixed, you're ready to go. Unlike most doughs, there is no proofing or rest period required before working with the dough. Roll out to approximately ⅛ inch thick and as square as possible; the square should be about 12 inches by 18 inches.

4. Stuff with your favorite filling, forming a long rope.

5. Roll up with enough dough to make about three layers, pinch and bake.

Note: Dough can last a few days in the refrigerator before it begins to oxidize.

To Make the Filling

1. Boil the potatoes for about 20–30 minutes. To check if the potatoes are done, take a chunk and press it with a spoon; if it easily smashes with no real resistance, they're done. Strain the potatoes into a large mixing bowl.

2. While still warm, smash the potatoes using either a large spoon or a potato masher until most of the big chunks are broken down.

3. While boiling the potatoes, in a large sauté pan, melt the butter over medium heat. Once the butter has melted, add the onions.

4. Cook the onions in the butter over medium heat till the onions start to turn translucent. Add salt and pepper to your onions.

5. Add your sweated onions and butter to the smashed potatoes. Mix them together until everything is incorporated. Taste to make sure your salt and pepper is appropriate; a heavy hand works best here.

Baking Information

After rolling out and portioning our knish, we like to brush ours with egg wash and sprinkle everything bagel spice on top for an extra burst of flavor. Place your topped knish on a sprayed baking sheet, making sure that the knish are not touching. Place the knish in a 400-degree oven and bake for 25–35 minutes (depending on your oven), rotating the tray halfway through cooking.

Chapter 10

CEREALSLY UPSTATE

What do a Progressive Christian physician and Woodstock have in common? It's not a trick question. They are both promoters of that earth-crunching, Birkenstock-wearing, tree-hugging food known as granola. What some view as a hippy-dippy health food was actually the creation of a progressive Christian physician in Dansville, New York. Dansville can be found in the town of Sparta, in the western region of New York state's Livingston County. Named for Daniel Faulkner, this tiny town that occupies less than three square miles was founded in 1795 as part of the land ceded by the Iroquois Nation after the Revolutionary War. Dansville is home to natural spring water that some have termed "All Healing" as it contains an enviable combination of minerals. This gift from Mother Nature made Dansville the perfect spot for what today we might term a wellness retreat. Back in the day, somewhere in the mid-1800s, that type of health spa, think Miraval meets Canyon Ranch, was called a sanitorium, and none had as high a profile as the one located in Dansville.

Spa Day

In 1890, the Jackson Sanitorium declared itself "the best-appointed health institution in America." The sanitorium, built in 1854, was administrated by Dr. James Caleb Jackson, who was part of a movement that touted the merits of hydropathy, a water-cure approach to medicine. The location was described by Bunnell and Quicks in their work detailing Dansville as "a special inducement to health seekers." It was only an eight-hour ride from New York City and twenty-four to Chicago by train. Not quite what today we'd call a day trip, but back then it was considered convenient. Jackson and his family were quite the legends in this part of New York. Born in Manlius, in Onondaga County, in 1811, he was a descendant of Colonel Giles Jackson, the chief of staff under General Gates at the Battle of Saratoga. Jackson graduated with his medical degree from the Medical College in Syracuse and practiced a holistic approach to medicine in Glen Haven by the Skaneateles Lake in Cayuga County.

Portrait of James Caleb Jackson. *National Library of Medicine.*

Trading on his medical degree, he and his family members invested $750 in the sanitorium. When he assumed the role as chief of staff, he renamed it Our Home on the Hillside. Atlas Obscura notes it became a place for patients to come and recuperate after a nervous breakdown. Think the *The White Lotus* without Jennifer Coolidge. It was there that Jackson created a unique approach to healing that was ahead of his time, relying on fruits, vegetables and unprocessed grains. This led him to blend bran and graham flour, which he would bake, break into small pieces and then bake again. He soaked the baked dough overnight in milk to make it more palatable and chewable. Jackson called this concoction granula. If Grape Nuts and graham crackers had a child, this would be it. Perhaps the name was a nod to the granular quality of the food, which is considered to be the very first dry breakfast cereal to be created in America. At its height of popularity, it sold for twenty cents a pound—that was, until a competitor brought his version to market.

It seems that one John Harvey Kellogg, yes that Kellogg, came to Dansville to learn from Jackson and became enamored of his granula.

Women at the Jackson Sanitorium enjoying a round of golf. *Library of Congress.*

Soon after, Kellogg established his health spa in Battle Creek, Michigan, where he coopted Jackson's dry cereal. After a heated legal battle, Kellogg had to brand his version as granola to distinguish it from Jackson's. Kellogg's version dominated the market as Jackson's brand of granula floundered. Jackson's later years were not a total decline into anonymity. The Home on the Hillside was the literal home to America's "Angel on the Battlefield" Clara Barton, as she lived there after experiencing considerable exhaustion. The Dansville Historical Society is quite proud that Dansville in turn became the first outpost of Clara Barton's Red Cross. If Jackson and the sanitorium are not instantly recognized for his creation of granula, he should be remembered for hosting speakers such as Elizabeth Cady Stanton, Susan B. Anthony and Frederick Douglass. He was an outspoken abolitionist, publisher and father of American dry cereal.

Granola-Rock Star

Now, let's find that thread between Jackson and Woodstock. You might recall a little music festival that took place in 1969 at Yasgur's Farm in

Bethel, Sullivan County, New York. The festival became known as Woodstock, which in reality was a town forty miles southwest in Ulster County. There, for three tumultuous days and nights, close to 500,000 young people gathered for a music festival featuring over thirty-two acts ranging from Jimi Hendrix to Joan Baez. The crowd was expected to be about 50,000 people, so as the rain deluged the dairy farm, the food and bathroom facilities were overrun by close to 400,000 attendees. How does that possibly bring us back to granola, you might wonder. With food being scarce and the local farms not being able to mobilize to meet the immediate demand, granola enjoyed its second act.

Michael Lang, festival promoter and author of *The Road to Woodstock*, recalled, "No one had ever handled food service for an event this size." He went on to write that before the opening day, he hired a local group called Food for Love to handle the concession stands. As food trucks ran out of provisions and concession stands that had been charging exorbitant prices had nothing left to sell, local commune members from what was called the Hog Farm came to the rescue. The Hog Farm was originally hired to provide security for the festival; the group was organized (I use the term loosely) by one Hugh Romney, who was better known as Wavy Gravy. You guessed it, Ben & Jerry's named an ice cream flavor as an homage to him. Members of the commune, seeing the food shortage urgency, prepared granola, which they scooped into cups and handed out to concertgoers. It's reported that Wavy Gravy stood on the stage on the Sunday morning of the event and announced to the crowd, "Breakfast in bed for 400,000." They then proceeded to hand out paper cups full of granola. Hence, the eternal association between granola, hippies and Upstate New York.

Advertisement poster for the 1969 Woodstock Music Festival. *Wikimedia Commons.*

SHREDDING THE WHEAT STORY

As long as we're on the sexy topic of dry cereal, we would be remiss to leave out Henry Perky, who has been called the father of shredded wheat—now there's an enviable title. Although not a native of Upstate New York, he made Watertown the epicenter of the cereal world. Known to have digestive issues, Perky, in 1892, traveled to Watertown to work with friend and machinist William H. Ford. Together they developed equipment to turn out Perky's concept, which he called "little whole wheat mattresses." Perky was searching for a manufacturing facility that reflected the wholesome nature of his product. Despite efforts by the Niagara Falls Power Company to entice him to their industrialized park, as outlined by Western New York historian Susan Eck, Perky decided to locate his plant in a residential area. Perky built a state-of-the-art factory that he called the Palace of Light. The complex sported tennis courts and a playground and cost a staggering $2 million to construct. He conceptualized the plant to be an all-inclusive facility to fulfill his vision of a better work-life balance. The cafeteria offered free lunches to female employees, while men paid ten cents for lunch composed of soup, shredded wheat toast, beef cutlets, baked potatoes, beet salad, Boston baked bread, Charlotte pudding and coffee. Speaking of coffee, Perky offered daily breaks for his employees, as did two other area factories, Larkin Soap and the Barcolo Company, both located in Buffalo. It is said that these companies were the first to offer a "coffee break" to their workers.

"Food fads" may come and go, but Shredded Wheat goes on forever.

The one breakfast food that survives the changing moods of public fancy is

Shredded Wheat

the food that shows up every year with in creased sales in spite of panics, industrial depression or competition.

The grocer who doesn't know something about the delicious dishes that can be made of Shredded Wheat Biscuit in combination with fruits is missing a great opportunity to please his customers.

We will spend more money this year than ever before to advertise Shredded Wheat and to make business for the retail dealers. Be ready to meet the increased demand by always carrying a good stock of the only breakfast cereal that has become a recognized staple.

Made only by
The Shredded Wheat Co.
Niagara Falls, N. Y.

Early advertisement by the West Company for the Shredded Wheat Company. *Wikimedia Commons.*

During the Pan-American Exposition, which coincided with the factory's opening, visitors to the area could tour the Natural Food Company factory and sample his shredded wheat and Triscuits. In a review of Perky's exhibit at the fair, the *Buffalo Courier* reported, "Over at the right a model kitchen with an electric range furnishes a place where daintily dressed and skillful cooks prepare shredded wheat into dishes that send forth tempting odors and arouse the interest of food epicures." Soon after, Perky was disassociated with the company and set his sights elsewhere; however, the company moved forward, renaming itself the Shredded Wheat Company. In 1908, the company began featuring images of Niagara Falls on its packaging. The company evolved into Nabisco Shredded Wheat, the name it is sold and marketed under today.

• • • • • • • • • •

Recipe: Homemade Granola

Jackson wasn't wrong that granola can be a very healthy part of your diet. When it contains whole grains, nuts and dried berries, it is delicious on top of yogurt or as a crunchy cereal for those with strong teeth.

4 cups old-fashioned rolled oats
1 cup nuts (rough chopped pecans or slivered almonds work well)
½ cup seeds (pepitas, sunflower)
½ cup unsweetened shredded coconut
½ teaspoon kosher salt
½ teaspoon ground cinnamon
½ cup melted coconut oil
½ cup neutral vegetable oil
¼ cup maple syrup
¼ cup honey
1 teaspoon vanilla extract
1 cup dried fruit (such as raisins, dried cranberries, dried pineapple, dried mango)

Preheat the oven to 350 degrees and line a large baking pan with parchment.

Toss together the first 6 ingredients, then add the oils, maple syrup, honey and vanilla. Toss thoroughly with your hands so the dry ingredients are completely coated with the wet.

Pour the mixture onto the baking pan and smooth out with a spatula. Bake for 20–30 minutes, stirring the granola every 10 minutes to prevent burning. Remove from the oven when the nutty aroma fills your kitchen and the ingredients are toasted to a medium brown. Let cool, then break up into clumps. Stir in the dried fruit and place in a sealed container.

Chapter 11

FISH STORIES

There's something fishy about Upstate New York. It would certainly stand to reason, as the region is overflowing with freshwater lakes and ponds, sports rivers and streams as well as portions of not one but two Great Lakes. This abundance of water creates an environment perfect for diverse aquatic plants and hundreds of species of fish. It also allows for some pretty interesting fish stories. There's the one about the two-headed trout in Roscoe, New York, and the reclusive eel trapper of Hancock. How about reports of sturgeon as large as fifteen feet long and weighing in at eight hundred pounds or salmon so eager to be caught they would jump clear out of the river into the hands and aprons of women waiting at the shores? These stories, some true, some a little less so, make for wonderful dinner conversation at one of New York's most prized rituals, Fish Fry Friday. Let's start with what we can verify and work our way upstream to the fish story we only wish was true.

Sweet Fish Story

The Salmon River, which earned its name, is home to Coho, Chinook and Atlantic salmon. As early as 1654, Jesuit Fathers Le Mercier and Le Moyne as well as explorer Samuel Champlain traveled the Oswego River, where they encountered Oneida Indians who had mastered the art of salmon fishing.

Artwork created by Wenceslaus Hollar in the 1600s to depict the abundance of salmon in New York waters. *University of Toronto Wenceslaus Hollar Digital Collection.*

They wrote, "With their canoes filled with fresh salmon…one of our men caught twenty large salmon on the way up the river.…There were so many of them that they were struck without difficulty." Other accounts describe salmon so abundant that farmers were spearing them with pitchforks and horses crossing streams would stomp on them underfoot. The Iroquois called the river Heh-hah-wa-gah, which means "where swim the sweet fish." Dwight A. Webster, professor of fishery science at Cornell, writes extensively about the preponderance of salmon in New York waters. It's estimated that skiff fishermen using only spears could catch thirty tons a year. By the 1800s, the supply had begun to dwindle, a result of pollution quite possibly from the development of the Erie Canal combined with overfishing the waters. Efforts were made in the early to mid-1900s to restock the river and have continued to this day. With an eye toward conservation, new regulations and taking better care of our natural resources, the Chinook, Coho and Atlantic salmon returned to the waters and are thriving. Much credit goes to the Salmon River Fish hatchery located outside of Pulaski in Altmar, which raises over three million salmon and trout a year to put back into the waters. It has resulted in the Salmon River becoming one of the top sportfishing areas in New York state. If you are angling for a fun autumn outing and possibly snagging your evening's dinner, try being an angler on the Salmon River; you just might catch a forty-five-pounder! You can then look to one of the area's inventive chefs to cook it up.

WHERE'S THE BEEF

In keeping with swordfish steak not being meat, welcome Albany beef into your food vernacular. This remnant term from the mid-1800s refers to sturgeon, a fish that was plentiful in the Hudson River. Back in the day, sturgeon and its prized fish roe known as caviar could be found in the waters of the Hudson. The river originally carried the name given to it by the Lenape, Muhheakunnuk (Mahicannituck), which means "river that flows two ways" or "waters that are never still." The name was usurped when Europeans settled the area and renamed the waterway for Henry Hudson, who explored the region in the 1600s. When Native Americans fished the

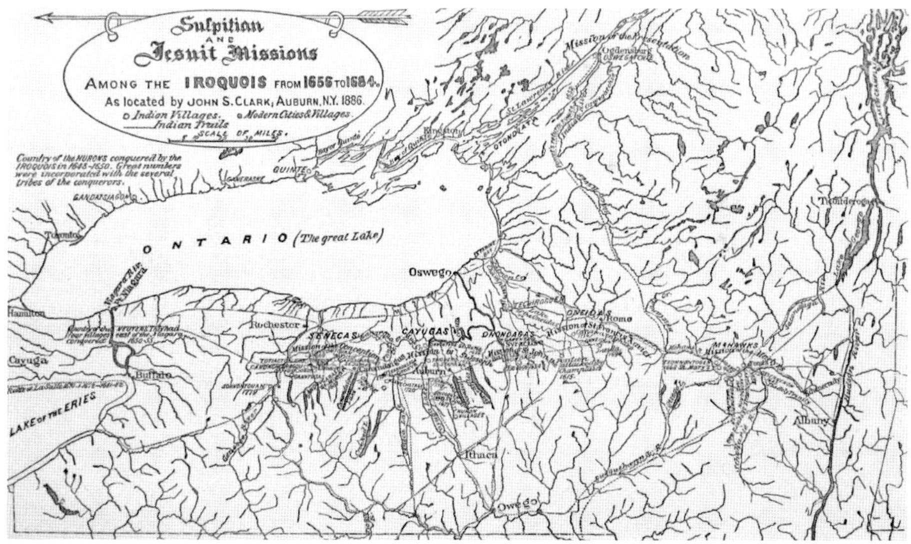

This 1886 illustration traces the travels of the Jesuit priests who traversed the region and interacted with the Native Nations. *Wikimedia Commons, Internet Archive Book Images, Shea, John Gilmary.*

An 1890 image of an enormous sturgeon leaping out of the water. *Courtesy of* Old Yonkers 1646–1922: A Page of History *by Brown, Henry Collins.*

river, it was plentiful, with everything from striped bass and shad to herring and oysters. The Hudson River led the way to the development of Upstate New York as an agricultural center, and impressive manor homes could be seen lining its shores. Most notable was Albany, where the government of New York centralized, and the city itself became known for the sturgeon that swam in its waters. Some could grow as large as fifteen feet and weigh as much as eight hundred pounds. Albany gained the nickname "Sturgeondom" or "Sturgeontown," and the residents in the mid-1800s were affectionately known as "Sturgeonites." A 1903 Rand McNally & Co. guide to the Hudson referred to "Albany beef" as "a pig, without a pig's obstinacy. He spends much of the time rooting and feeding in the mud at the bottom." It described the sturgeon fishermen with about as much reverence, citing them as having "an indolent, lazy time of it…they appear as if anchored and asleep." Industrialization along the river led to extreme pollution, and efforts by organizations such as Riverkeeper to control the damage done have created restrictions on fishing sturgeon. The once popular smoky flesh enjoyed by Albany residents in colonial times now needs to be purchased at an appetizing store rather than reeled in by a somewhat casual fisherman.

A SLIPPERY STORY

We now slip into that gray area that sounds more like food lore than fact, but if *National Geographic* is to be trusted, the eel trapper of Hancock, New York, is a very real person. For most, the eel would not be at the top of anyone's favorite fish list; its snakelike form and slippery skins make it seem more like a creature than a delicacy. That is, unless you live along the upper Delaware River where it merges at Hancock and the eel is a source of local pride. The lack of dams on the mainstream of the Delaware makes it possible for the eel to achieve upriver migration. The eel goes to a lot of effort to make its way Upstate. It begins its life in the Sargasso Sea and migrates to the Delaware River, where they are caught and harvested for local and European food markets. One local character rivals Rip Van Winkle in his solitary life and long white beard. That would be Ray Turner, who manages to turn river eels into a sweet and savory delicacy. Turner's Delaware Delicacies Smokehouse is a legendary shack where eel, brined in salt and honey, is then smoked over applewood and sold at the end of a dirt road off Route 17. Turner uses a contraption called a weir to trap the eel at the height of the season when they return to the river. The three-hundred-foot-long trap is painstakingly assembled and disassembled every season. A true authority on the eel, Turner noted in an NYup.com interview that on the first Thanksgiving, the eel was eaten more than turkey. So famous is this smoking Catskill eel trapper that he was featured in a 2015 episode on Nat Geo titled "Bloodworms, Eels & Gators." Next time you're in the Catskills and you have a hankering for smoked eel, follow the road signs nailed to a tree and discover a true local legend.

Two Heads Are Better Than One

Speaking of legends, we have reached the part where fact and fiction collide. That would be the legend of the two-headed trout at the junction of Beaverkill River and Willowemoc Creek River junction in Roscoe. The name conjures images of a mythical creature, and no doubt there is local folklore to match, but in reality, the two-headed trout earned its moniker quite simply. The story goes that the fish was in a quandary. Having reached the junction of these two lovely bodies of water, the trout, who was named Beamoc, did not know which direction to go. In a moment of indecisiveness, he sprouted two heads so that he could face both rivers and not have to choose one over the other. Beamoc is celebrated in Roscoe at what is called the two-headed trout dinner. Grab your rod and wade the waters; you just might be the first to catch Beamoc. If you do, be sure to throw him back.

A welcoming sign at Roscoe's information booth. Notice the bookended books and the title referencing Beamoc. *Wikimedia Commons, Kenneth C. Zirkel.*

With the abundance of fresh fish, it's no wonder Upstate New Yorkers have taken farm to table and turned it on its gills, perfecting water to plate. While roasted Coho salmon and smoked eel sound delicious, Upstate New Yorkers are partial to a good old-fashioned fish fry. In a tradition born from the observance of Lent, Catholics arriving from Italy, Ireland, Germany and Poland needed an inexpensive, readily available fish to take the sting out of giving up meat. What might have started as an act of piety quickly spread to local restaurants, and fish fry became a Lenten ritual. Fried fish is certainly not singular to this region, but residents of Central New York have elevated it to an art form. Now this tradition is repeated not just during Lent but other Friday nights as well. What fish is the choice of most restaurants? For Upstaters, that would be haddock. Haddock holds up well to frying, with a firm white flesh and a non-fishy taste. NYup.com reports that ironically haddock is not caught in New York waters. Upstate receives their supply fresh from Boston or more often frozen from Norway, and a supermarket can sell about three hundred pounds on a typical Friday, with double that number during Lent. Next time you think that Upstate is all about wings, remember it's about tails and gills too. It's the perfect place to wade the waters, navigate the streams, watch the salmon jump and enjoy fabulous fish spawned by the creative talents of local chefs. You also need to try out a Fish Fry Friday. Be sure to check out the "Where to Go" section at the back of the book for some more suggestions.

• • • • • • • • • •

Recipe: Fish Fry Friday

No need to wait for Friday to make this quick and delicious fried fish. Haddock is the choice of Upstate, but if your fishmonger does not have haddock, you can substitute cod or flounder. Using the corn muffin mix lends a touch of sweetness. I'm offering two versions, so you choose your favorite.

Serves: 4
Start to finish: Under 30 minutes

4 (6-ounce) pieces whitefish such as haddock, cod or flounder
1 egg beaten with a splash of milk
½ teaspoon kosher salt
¼ teaspoon black pepper
½ teaspoon garlic powder
½ teaspoon cayenne or chili powder, optional
½ cup corn muffin mix
¼ cup all-purpose flour
⅓ cup vegetable oil
2 tablespoons butter

Create a dredging station with the beaten egg and milk in one shallow bowl, seasoned with salt, pepper, garlic powder and cayenne or chili powder, if using, and the cornmeal mixed with the flour in another.

Heat the oil and butter until shimmering. Dip one piece of fish at a time in the cornmeal mixture, then in the egg wash, allowing the excess to drip off, then in the cornmeal mixture again. Gently place in the hot skillet and cook for about 3–4 minutes per side, or until nicely browned and cooked through. Repeat with the remaining pieces. If some of the fillets are very thick, you can continue cooking them in a warm oven for about 10 minutes. Serve with a squeeze of lemon or tartar sauce, recipe below.

If using breadcrumbs, do not mix them with the flour:

Fill one pan with the flour, one with the seasoned egg wash and a third with the breadcrumbs. Dip first in the flour, then the egg, then the breadcrumbs. Fry as directed above.

Tartar Sauce

½ cup mayonnaise
2 tablespoons sweet pickle relish
1 dill pickle, minced fine (about 2 tablespoons)
Squeeze of lemon or splash of vinegar, optional

Combine all the ingredients and chill.

Chapter 12

AN APPLE A DAY

It would be preposterous to suggest that Upstate New York was the first to grow an apple tree; we all know that credit goes to the Garden of Eden. However, New York currently ranks as the second-largest apple-producing state in the country after Washington. Wayne County is the epicenter of the apple industry by acreage in New York State, according to data from the U.S. Agriculture Census of 2017. Wayne sits snugly on the border of Lake Ontario's south shore and is considered to be part of the Rochester metropolitan area at the northern edge of the Finger Lakes. While New York State boasts over fifty thousand acres of apple orchards, Wayne accounts for almost half. According to *The History of Apples in Western New York*, featured on exploregeneseevalley.com, by Katie Sutor, the state grows close to thirty million bushels of apples a year. It joins the Hudson Valley and Champlain Valley as the heart of the New York

CORNELL UNIVERSITY.
AGRICULTURAL EXPERIMENT STATION OF
THE COLLEGE OF AGRICULTURE.
Department of Horticulture (Extension Work).

AN APPLE ORCHARD SURVEY
OF
WAYNE COUNTY, NEW YORK.

UNDER THE DIRECTION OF
JOHN CRAIG.

PART I — THE APPLE INDUSTRY, BY G. F. WARREN, Fellow in Agriculture.

PART II — GEOLOGY, BY W. E. McCOURT, Fellow in Geology.

ITHACA, N. Y.
PUBLISHED BY THE UNIVERSITY.

This expansive report shows the overwhelming importance of Wayne County in the study of apple orcharding. *Bulletin 226. Cornell University Agricultural Experiment Station.*

apple industry. You don't need a degree in pomology to see the conditions are ripe for apple growing in Upstate New York. However, Elizabeth Ryan, who holds that impressive degree, explains that the pH of the soil is ideal, the rolling hills and mountains afford drainage and the lake effect helps moderate the weather.

Big Red

The McIntosh Red apple (not to be confused with the Macintosh, which is the computer) is the apple of New York's eye, but it was not native to the state; the variety was brought here via Ontario, Canada, after it was discovered in 1811. In a case of name recognition, the New York State farmer who discovered the first seedling was none other than John McIntosh. Not afraid of cool nights, this hardy apple has thrived, as the climate and soil in Upstate New York is the perfect environment for this variety. It is joined by the Empire, Red Delicious, Cortland, Idared, Crispin and Rome, which also prosper in the region.

The first report on apples and the fruit's connection to Upstate, more specifically Western New York, involves a controversial figure, Asa Danforth. It seems this dubious character is most commonly associated with road development, possibly swindling Canada and several other unsavory activities. But one of his sweet contributions was bringing apple seeds with him back in 1748 when he settled in Onondaga County. Significant contributions were also made by horticulturist George Ellwanger, who settled in Rochester. He studied and labored in the nursery business (tending to crops, not infants). There he joined forces with fellow horticulturist Patrick Barry to create the Mount Hope Garden and Nurseries in Rochester. By 1888, it had become the largest nursery in the world! While they had acres of ornamental trees and shrubs, scattered vineyards and specimen trees, the bulk of their acreage was devoted to fruit trees. Ellwanger and Barry are credited with changing the nickname of Rochester from the "Flour City" to the "Flower City."

By the early to mid-1800s, orchards had begun to sprout in much of Upstate, especially along the band near Lake Ontario. Western New York History (wnyhistory.org) noted that in the 1880s, New York enjoyed a boom in the apple industry. This growth supported not only the farming community but also barrel makers, known as cooperages, and even basket makers were needed to meet the demand. In an October 6, 1876 article, the *Granville Sentinel* succinctly reported, "The farmers of this village are now

This photo taken in 1882 shows the hardworking laborers tending to what they termed "orcharding business." *New York State Agricultural Experiment Station.*

gathering their apple crop. They report the crop good." The best apples were for eating, the next best would be shipped out of state and those not deemed worthy were made into cider and vinegar. The commercialization was so intense that Heinz built a vinegar processing plant in Medina in 1899. One man, Clark Allis, stood out in the area. He was dubbed the "apple king" of Medina. Susan Eck, who wrote on the topic of Medina and apples, described Allis as being quite the multitasker. Not only did he have over 150 acres of apple orchards, but he also innovated cold storage facilities and had his own evaporator and an acetylene gas generator. He was such a progressive thinker that in 1906, he owned one of only twenty-six cars on the road in Medina. His impact continued through the early 1900s, dabbling in politics and entrepreneurship.

Variety Is the Spice of Life

The Hudson Valley also has a robust apple legacy as the birthplace of commercial orcharding. There's evidence that orchards existed in Ulster

County as early as 1671 and that land patents were created to attract the Scots and Irish to settle and farm the land. Early settlers included apples as part of their diets and preserved the fruit through the winter by storing them in insulated pits. A large portion of the crop was fermented into cider, with an average farmer stocking anywhere from twenty to fifty barrels each season. The most prolific varieties in the area were the Esopus Spitzenburg and the Jonathan. Ryan points out that many of the apples in the region have now been crossbred and given way to varieties such as the Jonagold and RubyFrost. Once again, Cornell has led the way in agricultural findings, and they can be credited with crosses such as the Cordera (Honeycrisp and Liberty), Luster (Honeycrisp and Gala) and Firecracker (Golden Delicious and Monroe and Melrose). The region, with help from local growers and Cornell, keeps creating new varieties to ensure Upstate New York is always outstanding in the field. According to Cornell University, Robert Livingston Pell, in the 1820s, planted the first commercial orchard in that region in Esopus, New York. Pell came from quite a lineage, with family members having signed the Articles of Confederation. He was not groomed to grow apples, attending a science and military academy and then Yale, but his heart was focused on the land and agriculture. His 1880 obituary in the *New York Times* praised his acumen with fruit trees, most specifically apples and

This shows an apple tree being grafted to produce a hybrid apple. *Wikimedia Commons, Karelj.*

peaches. In March of that same year, he was noted for his "apple fame" as the *Iron County Register* wrote, "He was the most successful man in this specialty in the world....The famous pippins have carried his name to a wide range of foreign parts....It will be a fortune to his heirs." The newspaper went on to describe the twenty thousand trees he had, which were derived from a few trees his grandfather obtained in Newtown, Long Island. The pippin's fame crossed oceans, as Ryan noted that Thomas Jefferson complained in a letter that he wrote while stationed in Paris: "They have no apples here to compare with our Newtown Pippin." It's also been reported that Ben Franklin received a shipment from New York and brought it to the royal court. Few other apples can claim such international fame.

Don't Waste a Drop

In a region that produces too many apples, you have several options as to what to do with the extras. You could host a William Tell archery contest, spend weeks on end bobbing or turn the apples into a deliciously refreshing tart and sweet drink known as apple cider. Happily, the industrious residents of Upstate New York chose the latter. Daniel Pucci plunged headfirst into the apple barrel in his book *American Cider* and uncovered some interesting facts about the cider of Upstate New York. First, let's discover the difference between the apple cider you pour for your children and the one you reserve for yourself. Hard cider has an alcoholic content, which is caused when yeast is added to the apple juice, converting the sugar into alcohol. It can also happen organically, which is how the cider industry in New York began. Without refrigeration, apple juice left unchilled would ferment. The result was hard cider that was drunk, and I use the term in all its connotations, by both adults and children. The hard cider was used to barter, as Edward Varno, the executive director of the Ontario Historical Society, noted: "For a barn raising, you might set out a barrel of whiskey or cider and pay your labor that way." Soon, cider mills sprang up to meet the demand. It just made sense; turning noneating apples into cider was practical and profitable. Although New York's cider was not as hardcore as some others where sugar was added to boost the alcohol content, most ciders ranged from 6 to 8 percent alcohol. Certainly enough to create a buzz and distract you from a Thanksgiving family feud. Drunkenness became problematic, as the temperance movement, which had deep roots in Upstate New York, took hold with pamphlets bemoaning the crisis. This 1827 example, written by a Canandaigua publisher, said, "While on earth, the victim of intemperance is as stupid as an ass, as ferocious as a tiger, as savage as a bear, as poisonous as the asp, as filthy as the swine, as fetid as the goat, and as malignant as a

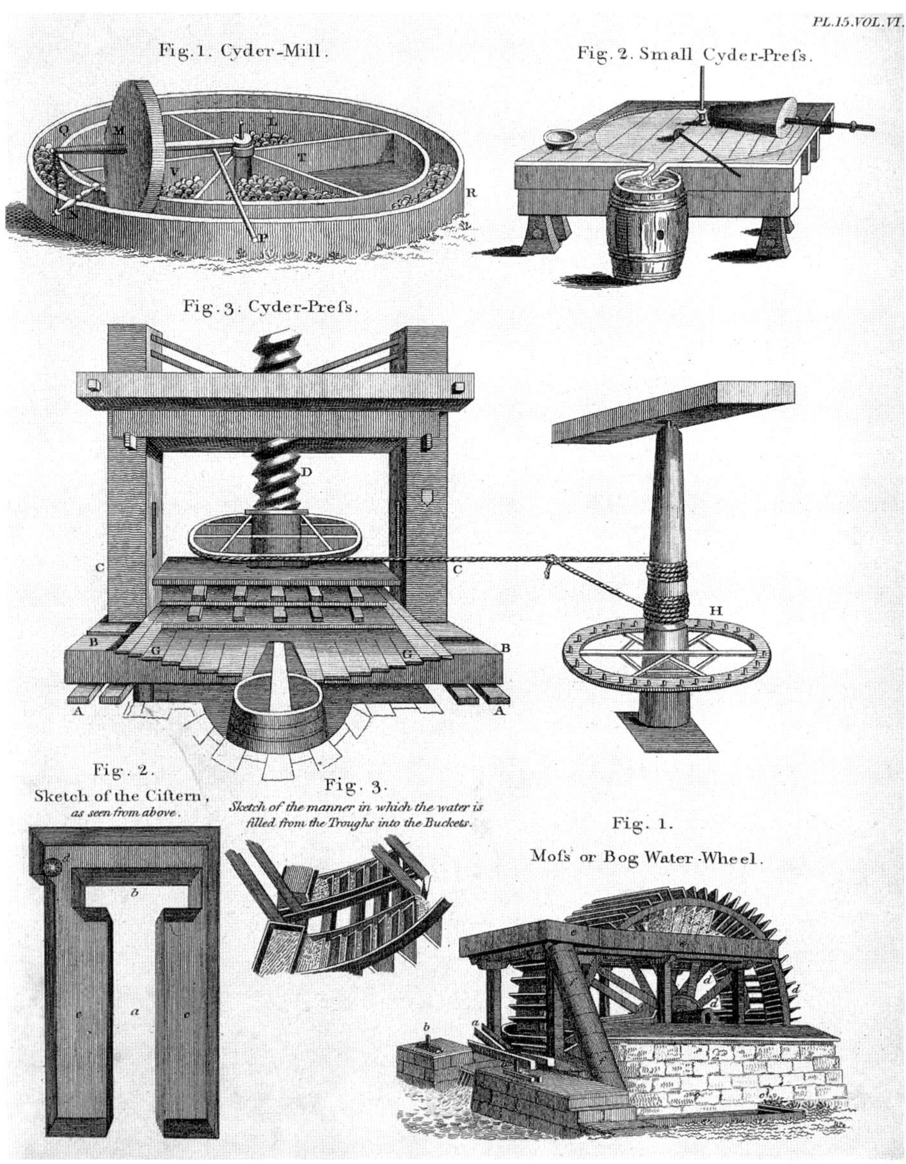

An engraving circa 1790 that shows the apparatus used to press apple cider. *Wellcomb Images.*

fiend." Another report of the effects of hard cider came in an 1833 case in Wayne County. There, a scuffle between neighbors, which made the Hatfield and McCoy issue seem tame, started:

> *He one day while at work in my father's field, got quite drunk on a composition of cider, molasses and water. Finding his legs to refuse their office he leaned upon the fence and hung for sometime; at length recovering again, he fell to scuffling with one of the workmen, who tore his shirt nearly off from him. His wife who was at our house on a visit, appeared very much grieved at his conduct, and to protect his back from the rays of the sun, and conceal his nakedness, threw her shawl over his shoulders.*

What makes that testimony ironically damning is the alleged drunk neighbor was Joseph Smith Jr., who went on to found the Church of Jesus Christ of Latter-day Saints. While Prohibition was not kind to the cider industry, people's preferences in beverages began to change, and the cider industry waned as a result. That's not to say that you can't get yourself a refreshing mug of cider in Upstate New York today.

Pucci focused on three regions to illustrate the nuances in Upstate cider. Citing the Hudson Valley, he found the character of the cider "is light and lean but ranges toward fuller textural with little to no bittersweet character." We know that the Hudson Valley favors apples such as Fuji, Gala, McIntosh and Macoun. So, the cider reflects those flavors. He noted the cider in the Finger Lakes tends to have a bitter/sharp component, with a high acid content and an alcohol content ranging from 7 percent ABV to 10 percent. Turning to New York's most prodigious apple-growing region, Western New York boasts a light and acidic cider made from varieties such as Cortlandt, Greening, McIntosh, Northern Spy and Honeycrisp. Whichever region you favor, you would be hard-pressed not to find some wonderful hard-pressed ciders to sample in Upstate New York.

Apples give way to apple tours, orchard picking and festivals throughout Upstate New York from the end of September through October. You can find everything apple-related, from homemade apple pie to apple dumplings, lessons on preparing apple butter and the freshest apple cider you've ever sampled. For some crisp apple-picking suggestions, visit the "Where to Go" section in the back of the book.

• • • • • • • • •

Recipe: New York State Fall Apple Sauce

Fresh apple sauce is just a few ingredients away. You control the sweetness and texture with just a few simple steps.

2 Granny Smith apples, about 1 pound, peeled, cored and cut into rough chunks
6 red apples, assorted varieties, about 3 pounds, peeled, cored and cut into rough chunks
1 cup New York State apple cider or apple juice
1 cinnamon stick
Brown sugar to taste
½ cup golden raisins, optional

Place the apples in a large saucepan and add the apple cider and cinnamon stick. Cover and cook over medium-low heat for 15 minutes. After that time, stir the apples with a wooden spoon and begin breaking up the larger chunks with the back of the spoon. Taste the collected juices, and if not sweet enough, add a bit of brown sugar. Reduce the heat to low, toss in the raisins if using and stir and check every few minutes until it reaches your desired consistency. Chill before serving.

Chapter 13

STRICTLY BUSINESS

Upstate New York lays claim to some lesser-known achievements; while they don't rival construction of the Erie Canal, they contributed to the culinary contributions of the region. Here's a quick rundown of some of those accomplishments.

JARRING

You would be correct if you assumed the Mason jar was called that because someone named Mason invented it. It's one thing to create a product; it's another to bring it to market. That's where Upstate New York comes in. Enter the Ball brothers, Edmund, Frank, George, Lucius and William, who, in 1880 bought the Wooden Jacket Can Company and began producing tin items suitable for storing and shipping paints, varnishes and oils. At the same time, they worked with a Poughkeepsie company to make glass inserts for their tin cans. Wanting complete control over

The industrious Ball brothers, *left to right*: William, Frank, Lucius, Edmund and George. *Ball State University Archives.*

production, they built a factory in Buffalo, and when the patent that Mason held expired, they began producing their glass jars, as did many other manufacturers at that time. A fire destroyed their New York factory, and they relocated to Indiana. Their association with Upstate ended, but Buffalo can still lay claim to being the site of their first successful endeavor.

IT'S IN THE BAG

Shifting from glass bottles to paper bags and Ball to Ballston, we discover George West, known lovingly as the Paper Bag King. Much like the Ball brothers, West didn't as much invent the paper bag as he promoted and developed it. Timothy Star, who truly wrote the book on West, called *The Paper Bag King*, noted that West was less an inventor and more a businessman; his strength was purchasing "promising paper bag patents," which gave him early access to the invention. West produced the bags in the Saratoga area, owning a dozen mills along the Kayaderosseras Creek. Considered a newfangled improvement over the cotton bags that were used at the time, West's bags were called "self-opened satchels," and by 1880 he was producing more than anyone else in the country.

CLEANUP ON AISLE 3

Every shopper has their favorite market, from their local grocer to the larger chains that make shopping fast and easy. But there's something special about Wegman's, an Upstate New York family market. Despite its size and considerable expansion, it has remained a family-owned and operated store since it first opened in Rochester in 1916. Wegman's was the first market to spray vaporized water on their produce, something you now see in every market and necessitates wearing a raincoat when you shop for produce. It also created a cafeteria space in the twenty-thousand-square-foot flagship store, which was unique to supermarkets at the time. Combining a philosophy of giving back to the local community by way of donating unsalable but wholesome food and being a forerunner of removing tobacco products from its shelves, Wegman's has set a standard for other markets and has ingratiated itself to the Rochester community.

The list of awards is as long as their dairy aisle, but it includes topping *Fortune* magazine's list of the one hundred best places to work, and *People* magazine's no. 1 ranking of its annual list of companies that care.

Spice It Up

Heintz & Weber, since 1922, has been relishing their footprint in South Buffalo, where they produce yellow mustard, pickled condiments and Buffalo's number-one-selling horseradish mustard. Trading the original slogan, "A pickle in the middle and Weber's on top," for their new catchphrase, "Everything's better with Weber's," the company is proud of its long association with Western New York.

This family-owned Buffalo-based company has provided more than eighty products to the country since the 1930s. *Courtesy of WeberMustard.com.*

QUEUING UP

What do you get when you combine killer barbecue and Harley Davidson motorcycle events? If you were three guys around Syracuse in the 1980s, the answer would be Dinosaur BBQ. Conceived as a food show on the road, according to their own PR, John Stage and his co-founders cut a fifty-five-gallon drum in half to create their first portable barbecue grill. They traveled up and down the East Coast and fed hordes of cult followers their barbecue at motorcycle shows, local fairs and festivals. Tired of the road, the owners settled in downtown Syracuse in 1988, where their barbecue joint gained an ever-larger following. They expanded to six locations, mainly in Upstate, and do a robust mail order and cookbook business. John credits their success to "staying committed to tradition but finding your own stamp and signature."

YOU'RE FULL OF BOLOGNA

Visit the website of the 125-year-old company Croghan Bologna, and you will be transported to a timeline so detailed that it tells what year the meat market opened (1871); when their ring bologna became a favorite in the lumber camps (1888); when a fire destroyed their Croghan shop (1912); what year the safe was robbed of one hundred dollars (1919); and even when a meat cutter injured his thumb, which by the way, became infected (1942). What it doesn't explicitly say is how important this Swiss-inspired ring bologna recipe is to the community that has enjoyed it for more than a century. Its smoky flavor, coarsely ground texture and shape that resembles salami or sausage make it a uniquely Upstate product, smoked over Adirondack wood and using locally sourced meat.

LET'S BE FRANK

How do you take a food of a questionable nature, such as the hotdog, and make it even less healthy? You dip it in a thick batter and deep-fry it. That's the magical carnival treat called the corndog, a food that gives nutritionists nightmares and carnival goers a thrill as exciting as a roller coaster; just don't eat one before riding one. The *New York Post* celebrated this American dream of a meal on a stick in a 2022 article and credits Buffalo businessman Stanley S. Jenkins as the innovator. Now, there's a real distinction in this citation. Jenkins most likely never sold a single corndog, but he did patent the machine that allowed others to do just that. His patent #US1706491S, filed in 1927 and approved in 1929, stated the following:

> *The present invention relates to cooking vessels and more particularly to an apparatus in which a new and novel edible food product may be deep fried… and consistin od* [sic] *an article of food impaled on a stic* [sic] *and coated with batter.…I have discovered that articles of food such, for instance, as*

It's not a state fair without a corndog stand, thanks Stanley! *Wikimedia Commons flickr, Steve Snodgrass.*

> *wieners, boiled ham, hard boiled eggs, cheese, sliced pineapples…,etc., when impaled on sticks and dipped in batter, which includes in its ingredients self-rising flour, and then deep fried in a vegetable oil at a temperature of about 390 F., the resultant food product on a stick for a handle is a clean, wholesome and tasty refreshment.*

Can we justly credit the inventor who facilitated the corndog's birth as the father of the corndog, even though he didn't stick around to raise it to the level it has achieved today? I believe so, as without his patented contraption, the corndog would remain an undiscovered treat, much to the dismay of the midway food vendor.

TO THE RESCUE

Should you overindulge in chicken riggies or have one too many slices of tomato pie, Upstate can lay claim to the antidote. The chalky bubblegum-pink combination of bismuth subsalicylate, zinc salt and phenyl salicylate that we lovingly refer to as Pepto-Bismol was marketed by Norwich Pharmacal in Norwich, New York's Chenango County. The ingredients in Pepto-Bismol had been around since the 1700s and were first brought to Norwich by a doctor who concocted a similar formula in his home. Unable to meet demand, the unnamed doctor turned his formula over to the pharmaceutical company, which tweaked the recipe. Sour stomachs have been thanking them for over one hundred years.

Chapter 14

THE SWEET SPOT

You've made it through the entire book to receive your just dessert. Let's discover Upstate New York's sweet side. Upstate New York is known for some pretty funky treats: turkey joints, peppermint pigs and sponge candy. Let's make it clear, no turkeys or pigs were harmed in the creation of those treats. The first is so named for its resemblance to the craggy bones of a turkey. If you've never had one, you should, as these inventions from Nora's Candy Shop in Rome, New York, are sugary sweet and delicious. To create the bone-like features, these six-inch-long candies have knobby knees created by nuts that are mixed into what

Were it not for the sign on the far left, you might easily drive right past Nora's, the home of turkey joints. *Google Maps.*

Nora's Candy Shop terms "chocolate marrow." Their coating has almost an eerie sheen from its silvery sugar coating. Nora's, which perfected the recipe, ships them seasonally from October through May. Much like the beloved New York cookie the Mallomar, it does not withstand the heat, so to avoid disappointment, they are simply not available in the warm weather. Today you can order them with a variety of nuts and centers from toasted almond and coconut to creamy peanut butter and their most popular, hazelnut.

Unlike its feathered friend, the peppermint pig looks like the animal it is named for. Created in Saratoga Springs and available at Christmas, these cheeky candies have become a holiday tradition. The bubblegum pink pigs have a hard candy shell molded to resemble a pig. The shape derives from a Victorian belief that the pig is a symbol of good health, happiness and prosperity. Or so reports the Saratoga Candy Company, which sells the trademarked candy. But eating this candy takes more than a firm grasp and a good overbite. The pig comes in a yuletide-inspired red box with a miniature hammer. A tradition dating back to the 1880s dictates that the pig, which was wrapped in a small cloth pouch, was passed to those who gathered. Each person would tap on the exterior, much as you would a piñata, with a long stick, but a little more gently. Once the pig cracked open, everyone would share a piece of the good fortune. Saratoga Sweets is to peppermint pigs what the North Pole is to gift giving. As the epicenter of this seasonal treat, Mike Fitzgerald brought this nineteenth-century tradition back to Saratoga in 1988. He shared with Yahoo News in 2012 they shipped about 130,000 of the treats. The candy is straightforward enough, pink-tinged sugar mixed with corn syrup to create the hard candy shell, which is poured into a pig-shaped mold. The small versions weigh in at about three ounces, with the largest, named Clarence, topping one pound. Take that, candy cane!

This brings us to sponge candy, which is neither shaped like an animal nor related to the item it is named for. The sponge refers to the soft center of the candy made popular in Buffalo and celebrated there annually on September 21. So, what exactly is it? Some describe the center as a caramelized spun sugar, others more like a honeycomb toffee. Everyone agrees that the airy center is then encased in a rich chocolate shell for delicious results. While Western New York is not the only place you can buy sponge candy, tradition dictates it's the only place you should buy sponge candy. Joseph A. Fowler is credited with bringing this confection to Buffalo. Upon arriving in 1901 to attend the Pan-American Exposition, Fowler

As the box boasts, Fowler's Sponge Candy has a one-hundred-plus-year history and is Buffalo's favorite sponge candy. *Courtesy of Fowler's Chocolates.*

established himself as a candymaker. There, at the exposition, he sold his handmade sweets. Shortly after, he opened his first store in the heart of Buffalo. These chocolatiers, similar to Mouseketeers but without funny hats, use chocolate and cocoa that has at least 60 percent cacao solids. Good quality cacao, which derives from the Greek meaning "food of the gods," makes for the best-finished product. Rich on the outside, tender on the inside, sponge candy might just give wings a run for their money as Buffalo's best food find.

You're a Lifesaver

Upstate New Yorkers haven't just created kitschy seasonal treats; they're also responsible for one of the world's favorite candies, the Lifesaver. Edward Noble of Gouverneur, New York, didn't so much invent Lifesavers, but he was the driving force behind what the Gouverneur Museum calls perforated candy. Noble approached candymaker Clarence Crane to market his peppermint treat. Instead of partnering with Noble, Crane sold Noble the business in 1913 for a reported $2,900. It was Noble, a resident of Gouverneur in St. Lawrence County, who wrapped the peppermints in tinfoil and then recruited a young salesforce to sell the candy across the country. The company launched the fruit-flavored rings in 1929, with the five-flavor pack still made today containing lemon, lime, orange, pineapple and cherry. Everyone had their favorite flavor and the one they would always happily share. So popular were the candies that during World War II, according to the museum, "23 million boxes of lifesavers were packed into military field rations allowing G.I.s to introduce the candy to foreign lands." Noble was truly a son of Upstate New York, as he both worked and played throughout the region, boating on the St. Lawrence, summering in the Thousand Islands and endowing hospitals, libraries and churches

This ad touts the benefits of Smith Brothers cough drops, a Poughkeepsie institution. *Courtesy of SmithBrothers.co.*

throughout the state. Take a drive to Gouverneur, and you'll be greeted by a larger-than-life statue of pep-o-mint Lifesavers donated as an homage to Noble.

Brotherly Love

Before we leave the candy store, it should be mentioned that the Smith Brothers of cough drop fame were Upstaters. Hailing from Poughkeepsie in 1847, William and Andrew, those bearded brothers, brewed the first batch of what they called "wild cherry cough candy." They didn't create the cough drop recipe, but they tweaked it to include, as their company website says, "candy-like flavors." To prevent knockoffs, in 1872, the brothers began packaging the drops in branded trademarked boxes. Hvmag.com credits the brothers for infusing the scent of licorice into Upstate air, as in 1915, they expanded their footprint to Church Street and increased production to six tons of drops a day. The company remained in Poughkeepsie for four generations until a Chicago firm coughed up the revenue to purchase the brand, at which time the plant was closed down.

Ooh La-La

If possibly creating the ice cream sundae was not enough to earn Upstate New York a place in the sweet spot hall of fame, enter apple pie à la mode. "À la mode" is the ooh-la-la French way of saying "of the day," and it was a fashionable phrase in the late 1800s. While there is more than one origin story, many, including the *New York Almanack*, attribute its inception to the Cambridge Hotel in Washington County, New York, a small town in the Adirondack Mountains. The story goes that in 1896, a music teacher named Professor Charles Watson Townsend, who was a regular at the hotel, would routinely order a slice of apple pie with a scoop of ice cream on the side. Mrs. Berry Hall, who was an employee at the hotel, dubbed it pie à la mode, and the name stuck. Soon after, Townsend dined at Delmonico's, a swanky restaurant in New York City. Thinking this dish was nationally known, he ordered it for dessert. When he was met with a confused stare Townsend was heard to say, "Do you mean to tell me that so famous an eating place as Delmonico's has never heard of Pie a la Mode, when the Hotel Cambridge, up in the village of Cambridge, NY serves it every day. Call the manager at once, I demand as good service here as I get in Cambridge." A reporter from the *New York Sun* overheard the entire exchange, and the news soon spread. Wouldn't you know, the next day, pie à la mode appeared on Delmonico's menu.

J-E-L-L-OH

Everyone knows there's always room for Jell-O, hence its inclusion at the end of this chapter. But I'm not sure that everyone knows that Jell-O is a very New York creation. Gelatin has been around for centuries, and its ability to freeze food in time with a jellied effect was often reserved for the upper-class elite, as the process of creating gelatin was time-consuming and expensive. Flash forward to 1845 in New York, when Peter Cooper, a jack of all trades, patented a powder he called "portable gelatin." According to New York's Jell-O Museum, his idea just didn't "jell." His product was not fully realized until 1897, as Andrew F. Smith related in the *Oxford Encyclopedia of Food and Drink in America*, when Pearl Waite, a carpenter and cough syrup manufacturer in LeRoy, New York, changed its trajectory. While Cooper created this easy-to-use gelatin, it was Waite who decided to flavor it, add color

Portrait of Pearle Bixby Wait (1873–1915). *Wikimedia Commons.*

and create what is now a ubiquitous dessert. It was Waite's wife, May, who coined the name Jell-O. As odd as it might sound, at the time, adding an -O to the end of a word was in fashion. After unsuccessfully marketing the product for two years, they sold the patent to Francis Woodward for a mere $450. He produced a health drink known as Grain-O. Trying to pinpoint why the product was not catching on, Woodward realized that home cooks were not accustomed to ready-made foods. Woodward promoted the product from his Genesee Pure Food Company in 1902 with recipe booklets, which he delivered door to door. His print ads featured a little girl delighted by Jell-O, even tapping famed illustrator Norman Rockwell to create one. By 1923, Genesee had become known as the Jell-O company, and two years later it merged with Postum Cereal Inc., the company that would become Kraft/General Foods. If you can't get enough of the Jell-O history, you should head to LeRoy's Jell-O Museum, where the Jell-O brick Road leads you down Main Street. Here are some fast fun facts courtesy of the museum.

The first four Jell-O flavors were orange, lemon, strawberry and raspberry.

During an airshow at the Woodward airport, pilots landed the plane, ate a bowl of Jell-O and then took off again.

Not all fruits float in Jell-O; the best picks are fresh fruits like apples, bananas, peaches, pears, oranges and grapefruit.

Salt Lake City consumes more lime-flavored gelatin than any other city in the United States.

Jell-O was described on its first label as "Delicate, Delightful and Dainty."

WHERE TO GO

This is the section that I have a love-hate relationship with. I love to shine a light on great spots to put on your Upstate food bucket list, but I hate that I can't list every single one. This section is designed to highlight the places that have been popularized over the years and have stood the test of time in addition to some newcomers who are getting lots of attention and deserve to be mentioned. If I list a place for one food, I won't list it again even if it excels in another category, as I try to focus on one specialty.

For information on local attractions, best to go to the site associated with that place. For instance, if you're looking for a wine tour in the Finger Lakes, google just that and you'll get specific references; looking to fish for Beamoc, google it and it'll take you there. This list is a good start, but there is so much to discover.

I'd love to make this list fluid, so if you have a spot you'd want to add, email me and I will post it on social media as well as my website. Feel free to send me photos of you at the establishments and I'll post those as well. I'm as sturdy as a beef on weck, with a thicker skin than salt potatoes, so feel free to weigh in on my selections; together we can create the ultimate Where to Go list.

Chapter 1. The First New Yorkers

This is a list of reliable sites that can help you discover the rich history of the Native American influence on Upstate New York.

Ganondagan State Historic Site: https://www.ganondagan.org/
Seneca Iroquois National Museum: https://www.senecamuseum.org/
Akwesasne Cultural Center and Museum: https://akwesasneculturalcenter.org/
National Shrine of Kateri Tekakwitha: https://www.katerishrine.org/
Onondaga Historical Association: https://www.cnyhistory.org/
Cayuga Museum of History and Art: https://cayugamuseum.org/
Iroquois Museum: https://www.iroquoismuseum.org/
Indian Ladder Trail: https://www.scenichudson.org/explore-the-valley/outdoor-adventures/adventure/indian-ladder-farms/

Chapter 2. Upstate's Greatest Hits

If I were to include every establishment that serves these iconic dishes, you would eat out every night and never prepare a home-cooked meal again. Instead, I focused on the places where the dish was born or immortalized to help keep it somewhat manageable.

Beef on Weck in Western New York

Anderson's
Bar Bill Tavern
Beef 'N' Barrel
Buffalo Brew Pub
Charlie the Butchers
Eckl's @Larkin
Glen Park Tavern
Schwabl's
Steve's Pig and Ox Roast
Swiston's Beef & Keg
Ulrich's Tavern

Buffalo Wings in Buffalo

Anchor Bar
Blackthorn
Cole's Restaurant & Pub
Doc Sullivan's
Duff's
Elmo's Bar & Restaurant
Gabriel's Gate
Gene McCarthy's
Mammoser's
Nine-Eleven Tavern

Chicken Riggies in Utica and Rome

Babe's
Bella Regina
Chesterfields
Daniele's
Delmonico's
It's a Utica Thing (sauce)
Venice Pizzeria
Ventura's
Teddy's

Garbage Plate: Rochester Area

Bill Gray's
Charlie's (Riedel's)
Dog Town Hots
Henrietta Hots
Jimmy Z's
Mark's
Nick Tahou Hots
Red Fern (vegan)
Schaller's
Steve T's

Grape Pie in and Around Naples

Arbor Hill Grapery & Winery
Cindy's Grape Pies
Heart 'N Hand
Jeni's Pies

Half Moon Cookies in the Utica Area

Dunn's Bakery
Harrison Bakery
Hemstrought's
Holland Farms

Best Burger in and Around Hamburg

Buffalo Bros Burgers
Juicy Burger Bar
Lucia's on the Lake
Poppyseed Restaurant
Ted's Hotdogs
Uncle Joe's Diner
Waterstone Grill

Hotdogs

Clare & Carl's
Dogtown
Famous Lunch
Gus's
Hotdog Charlie's
Lou's
McSweeney's
Mike's
Newest Lunch
New Way Lunch

Ronnie's Michigan Stand
Texas Red Hots

Tomato Pie in and Around Utica/Rome

Danielle's
Napoli's Italian Bakery
Roma

Upside Down Pizza

O'Scugnizzo's

Rolled Pizza

Sergi's

Salt Potatoes

Bull & Bear Roadhouse
Syracuse Salt Potatoes

Spiedies in Binghamton

Binghamton Hots
Lupo's
Sharkey's
Spiedie & Rib Pit

Utica Greens in Utica/Rome

Chesterfield
Georgio's Village Café

HONORABLE MENTION

Cornell Chicken

Brooks Barbecue
The Chicken Coop at the State Fair

Maple Syrup

Adirondack Maple Farms
New York State Maple Weekend

Bologna

Café Mutton

Chicken French: Rochester

Lemoncello
Monroe's
Mr. Dominic's
Pasta Villa
Phillips European Village
Proietti's

Chicken Finger Subs: Buffalo

Jim's Steakout
John and Mary's
John's Pizza and Subs
Lockport Gulf
Mayback's Deli
Mike's Subs

Spaghetti Parmesan: Buffalo

Chef's Restaurant

Stuffed Banana Peppers: Buffalo

Bobby J's Italian American Grille

Chapter 3. Festivals, Fairs and Food

Visit the regional websites for the best-updated information as well as these informative sites:

Discover Upstate New York: https://www.discoverupstateny.com/
Fairs and Festivals: https://www.fairsandfestivals.net/
Festival Guides and Reviews: https://festivalguidesandreviews.com/
I Love NY: https://www.iloveny.com/
New York Fall Foliage Guide: https://www.nyfallfoliage.com/
NYUP: https://www.newyorkupstate.com/
Taste NY: https://taste.ny.gov/

Chapter 4. The Canal's Culinary Culture

The Erie Canal: https://eriecanal.org/
Erie Canal Museum: https://eriecanalmuseum.org/
Erie Canalway: https://eriecanalway.org/
New York State Canal System: https://www.canals.ny.gov/

Chapter 5. Hangry at the Pan

Buffalo AKG Art Museum: https://buffaloakg.org/
The Buffalo History Museum: https://buffalohistory.org/

Historic Buffalo Art: https://www.historicpictoric.com
The Pan-American Exposition at Buffalo in 1901: https://panam1901.org/
University at Buffalo Digital Collections: https://digital.lib.buffalo.edu/

Chapter 6. Udderly Upstate

Dairy History

Cornell College of Agriculture and Life Sciences: https://cals.cornell.edu/
Historic Geneva: https://historicgeneva.org/
Little Falls Historical Society Museum: https://littlefallshistoricalsociety.org/

Cheese and More

Chaseholm Farm
Coach Farm
Four Fat Fowl
Maple Hill
Nettle Meadow Farm & Cheese
Old Chatham Creamery
Ronnybrook dairy farm

Ice Cream and Frozen Custard

Abbott's
Anderson's Frozen Custard
Custard's Last Stand
Donnelly's
Glen Dairy Bar
Grand Central Creamery
Harrigan's
Jones Humdinger
Kurver Kreme
Martha's Dandee Crème
The Penguin

Polar Bear
Purity
Seneca Farms
Sno Top
The Snow Man
Spotted Duck Creamery

Chapter 7. Drinking Up New York

Benmarl
Boundary Breaks
Brotherhood
Dr. Konstantin Frank Winery
Hermann Wiemer
Ravines
Red Newt
Red Tail
Vineyard View
Whitecliff

Breweries

Discover Upstate New York: https://www.discoverupstateny.com/
Inside + Out: https://insideandoutupstateny.com/
NYUP: https://www.newyorkupstate.com/
Times Union: https://www.timesunion.com/

Cocktail History

Tour with Kitty Hustler: https://www.hustlerstavern.com/

Wine/Cheese Trails

Explore the regional websites for the location you are visiting:

Explore Finger Lakes: https://www.fingerlakes.org/
New York Wines: https://newyorkwines.org/
NYUP: https://www.newyorkupstate.com/
Seneca Lake Wine Trail: https://senecalakewine.com/

Chapter 8. Health, History and Horses

Discover Saratoga: https://www.discoversaratoga.org/
Saratoga: https://www.saratoga.com/
Saratoga Mineral Water Tours: https://saratogamineralwatertours.com/
Saratoga Springs, NY: https://saratoga-springs.org/
Saratoga Spring Water: https://www.saratogawater.com/

Chapter 9. Let's Go to the Mountains

Catskills Borscht Belt Museum: https://www.borschtbeltmuseum.org/

Here Are Some Places to Stay in the Hudson Valley/Catskills

Benton House at Troutbeck
Bluebird Hunter Lodge
Camptown Catskills
Chatwal Lodge
Eastwind Oliverea Valley
Emerson
Hotel Lilien
Inness
Kenoza Hall
Mohonk

Resorts World
Wildflower Farms
Wylder Windham

Chapter 10. Cerealsly Upstate

Bethel Woods Center for the Arts: https://www.bethelwoodscenter.org/
Woodstock Museum: https://www.woodstockmuseum.com/

Chapter 11. Fish Stories

Discover some great fishing locations:

Bassmaster: https://www.bassmaster.com/
New York State Department of Environmental Conservation: https://dec.ny.gov/
On the Water: https://onthewater.com/

Fish Fry

Ankers
Doug's
Eddie F's
Rockland House
Smoked Eel: Ray Turner 607-637-4443
Ted's

Chapter 12. An Apple a Day

Apple Dave's
Apple Ridge
Barton Orchards

Beak and Skiff
Boehm Farms
Fishkill Farms
Dubois
Hurds
Kelder
Lawrence Farms
Prospect Hills

Cider

Angry Orchard
Bellwether
Cider Creek
World Cider Map: https://ciderguide.com/

Chapter 14. The Sweet Spot

Althea's Chocolates (sponge candy)
Antoinette's Sweets (sponge candy)
Gouverneur Museum (Lifesavers)
Jell-O Gallery: https://jellogallery.org/
Joseph A. Fowler (sponge candy)
Ko-Ed (sponge candy)
Nora's Candy Shop (turkey joints)
Park Edge Sweet Shoppe (sponge candy)
Saratoga Candy Company (peppermint pigs)
Sweet Jenny's (sponge candy)
Watson's (sponge candy)

BIBLIOGRAPHY

Bangs, Jeremy Dupertuis. *The Travels of Elkanah Watson*. McFarland, 2015.

Bovino, Arthur. *Buffalo Everything: A Guide to Eating in "The Nickel City"*. Countryman Press, 2018.

Burford, Peter. *Wines of the Finger Lakes*. Burford Books, 2016.

Cayleff, Susan. *Wash and Be Healed: The Water-Cured Movement and Women's Health.* Temple University Press, 1991.

Cazentre, Don. *Spirits & Cocktails of Upstate New York.* The History Press, 2017.

Cianciola, Nate. *Frenching Food Italian Style*. Lulu.com, 2006.

Dawson, Evan. *Summer in a Glass: The Coming of Age in Winemaking in the Finger Lakes.* Union Square & Co., 2012.

Falk, Laura Winter. *Culinary History of the Finger Lakes*. The History Press, 2014.

Federal Writers' Project. *New York: A Guide to the Empire State*. 1954.

Gibb, James, David Bernstein and Stephen Zipp. "Farm and Factory: Agricultural Production Strategies and the Cheese and Butter Industry." *Historical Archeology* 43, no. 2 (Spring 2009).

Goldwyn, Craig. *Meathead: The Science of Great Barbecue and Grilling.* Harvest, 2016.

Hedrick, U.P. *A History of Agriculture in the State of New York.* New York State Agriculture Society, 1933.

Hersh, June. *Iconic New York Jewish Food*. The History Press, 2023.

Ingersoll, Ernest. *Rand, McNally & Co. Illustrated Guide to the Hudson River and Catskill Mountains.* Rand, McNally & Co., 1903.

Lang, Michael. *The Road to Woodstoc*k. Ecco Books, 2010.

Leary, Thomas, and Elizabeth Sholes. *Buffalo's Pan American Exposition*. Arcadia Publishing, 1998.

McDonough, Patsy. *McDonough's Bar-Keepers' Guide and Gentlemen's Sideboard Companion*. Forgotten Books, 2018.

Meisel, Susan, and Nathalie Sann. *Fresh from the Farm*. Rizzoli International Publications, 2010.

Miller, Elizabeth Smith. *In the Kitchen.* Forgotten Books, 2018.

1940 NY State Historical Association. *New York, American Guide Series.* Oxford University Press, 1940.

Pinney, Thomas. *A History of Wine in America*. University of California Press, 2007.

Pucci, Daniel. *American Cider: A Modern Guide to a Historic Beverage*. Ballantine Books, 2021.

Rydell, Robert. *All the World's a Fair*. University of Chicago Press, 1987.

Silverman, Stephen, and Raphael D. Silver. *The Catskills: Its History and How It Changed America*. Knopf, 2015.

Smith, Andrew F. *The Oxford Encyclopedia of Food and Drink in America*. Oxford University Press, 2013.

Starr, Timothy. *The Paper Bag King*: *A Biography of George West*. Kindle, 2013.

Stewart, Mark. *New York Native Peoples*. Heinemann Library, 2008.

Willard, Xerxes Addison. *Dairy Farming*. C. Van Benthuysen, 1862.

Wondrich, David. *Imbibe!*. TarcherPerigee, 2015.

Websites

Albany: https://www.albany.com/

Albany Institute of History & Art: https://www.albanyinstitute.org/

Atlas Obscura: https://www.atlasobscura.com/

Buffalo Wing Festival: https://buffalowing.com/

Cornell College of Agriculture and Life Sciences: https://cals.cornell.edu/

Culture: https://culturecheesemag.com

Eden Corn Festival: https://edencornfest.com/

The Erie Canal Museum: https://eriecanalmuseum.org/erie-eats/

The Food Timeline: https://www.foodtimeline.org/

Ganondagan: https://www.ganondagan.org/

Genesee Valley: https://exploregeneseevalley.com

Hudson Valley Garlic Festival: https://www.hvgf.org/

Ithaca: https://www.ithaca.com/

Little Falls Historical Society Museum: https://littlefallshistoricalsociety.org/

Naples Grape Festival: https://naplesgrapefest.org/

Neversink Valley Museum of History & Innovation: https://neversinkmuseum.org/
New York Almanack: https://www.newyorkalmanack.com/
New York State Dairy Statistics: https://agriculture.ny.gov/system/files/documents/2023/09/2022dairystatisticsannualsummary.pdf
NYS Maples Producers' Association: https://nysmaple.com/
The Pan-American Exposition at Buffalo in 1901: https://panam1901.org/
Phelps, NY Sauerkraut Weekend: https://phelpsny.com/sauerkraut-weekend
Spiedie Fest: https://www.spiediefest.com/
Taste of Hamburger Festival: https://www.tasteofhamburger.com/
Utica University Ethnic Heritage Studies Center: https://www.utica.edu/directory/ethnic-heritage-studies-center
Western New York History: https://wnyhistory.org/
What's Cooking America: https://whatscookingamerica.net/
WIBX: https://wibx950.com/

ABOUT THE AUTHOR

June Hersh is a former teacher and businesswoman who began her food writing career after retiring in 2004. She is the author of *Recipes Remembered: A Celebration of Survival* (Ruder Finn, 2011), *The Kosher Carnivore* (St. Martin's Press, 2011), *Yoghurt: A Global History* (Reaktion Books, 2021), available in English, Arabic, Chinese and Japanese, *Iconic New York Jewish Food: A History and Guide with Recipes* (The History Press, 2023) and *Food, Hope & Resilience: Authentic Recipes and Remarkable Stories from Holocaust Survivors* (The History Press, 2023). Hersh served as editor and interviewer for *Still Here: Inspiration from Survivors and Liberators of the Holocaust* (www.stillherebook.com). She is currently working on a new book with Chef Alon Shaya focusing on stories from World War II through the lens of food. The book should be released in the fall of 2026. June's books have a charitable flavor, as her proceeds benefit various not-for-profit organizations and institutions. She speaks across the country on the topic of the Holocaust and food history. Her books are available on her website (www.junehersh.com) and other online booksellers. June resides in New York with her husband of forty-nine years and their adorable Bernedoodle, Mallomar.